# SKYBURST POLICE DEPT.

LeeAnn

authorHOUSE®

AuthorHouse™
1663 Liberty Drive, Suite 200
Bloomington, IN 47403
www.authorhouse.com
Phone: 1-800-839-8640

First published by AuthorHouse 2/20/2008

ISBN: 978-1-4343-5812-7 (sc)

Printed in the United States of America
Bloomington, Indiana
This book is printed on acid-free paper.

# THE STORY STARTS OUT WITH
# THE EMPLOYMENT OF THE AUTHOR

I AM INTENDING TO start a new career and this story is about the corruption at the police department that I run into. The cause and effect of working at Skyburst police department is so shocking that even some of the local police in the department are stunned.

This does not involve just one station in this county but several stations and the corruption that occurs and the effects it can and does have on the author is astounding.

The time it takes for the effect to have is many years and even though Lee Ann try's to hold on she is confronted with outside personal that cause even more damage and eventually her career is taken away from her.

Lee Ann and others go through things together when it is really not related to Skyburst P.D. she is found to have to endure it from even her family and friends and the way they treat her.

The situation even her man who she is so much in love with, the way it started was a fairy tale affair and the hurt and turmoil he places on her.

If you have any doubts of this then, you must realize the story as it involves corruption and believe me it all is true for I am Lee- Ann the Author.

If you have a hard time believing me the author than just think of the Move the Burning Bed with Farah Faucet, and the movie in which the man eventually after stalking his ex wife, and then having restraining orders, and the police not willing to enforce or keep him away, eventually stabbed her in front of her child and then jumped on her head in front of the police officer who eventually took the knife and put it in the trunk of the car and then tried to secure the ex wife and it was found that had the officer call for backup the ex wife would not have been left with the right side or her body working with the signal from her brain to the left side and her left side had no direction. Will you believe now that this is a true story and that I have chosen to use it for an example? This movie was aired on Lifetime TV station and reported it to be true. The Police there were all charged with one form of corruption or another. And had to pay a substantial amount of money to the ex wife for failure to keep him away from her.

Think about the way the officers did what they wanted, when they wanted and to whom they wanted. And the actually got away with it just because they are cops.

Don't forget the sexual harassment cases that Lee Ann had to go threw for ten years, the touching of her when ever they wanted. Then the sugar in the tank. The loss of her home and the illness's she was and still is forced to endure. Believe this author when she tells's you this really did occur.

Remember she is disabled now and has this Boy friend that she is not sure of where she stands. The son she and her boyfriend were to adopt together, that he now has and what he said about her then and now says something different.

Think about this that she was to have this child and know the child when in reality she has only seen a few pictures of him. But yet the Boy friend wants her to be responsible for this child should any thing happen to the boyfriend.

God Forbid that any does happen to the Boyfriend but can you imagine the audacity of the Boy friend to assume that she can just walk up to the child and take over his life at what ever age it would be required for her to do so when this child has never meet her. After there has been a nanny involved from the start. Pay attention to the many accidents she was involved in and how they have now left her disabled.

# I Would like to Express My Many Thanks to All Who Have Helped in the Production of this Book.

CAN YOU SAY THERE IS JUSTICE FOR ALL?

While I worked for the Skyburst Police Department for 181/2 years during which time I also worked at several second job's for most of these years as The Police Department just did not pay the bills by its self.

In the Year 2001, I have had my world entirely turned upside down and the cause of it is pretty shocking. I was introduced to a person who claimed to be an attorney and who worked out of a bank where he was impersonating an attorney under a disbarred attorney's license that he copied the license and changed the name on the license to carry out his fraud. There was a lack of communication due to Spanish speaking employees because I do not speak Spanish at all.

I lived in the district of Skyburst Police Department when I started for them. And I eventually moved to another county but I still worked for the Skyburst Department. During these years I received numerous commendations from my departments and other agencies.

I taught classes to sworn and non sworn personal. I also taught illiterate people how to read on a volunteer basis at the local library.

During my years with the department I had to put up with a lot of Harassment from the offices at the department. The types ranged from being followed around the office and outside employment, to being fondled and followed to my sister's home. Because I have to ware special shoes I was abused for this as well.

This year I was set up by this so called attorney to type applications to seal criminal records. I was supposed to get paid $100.00 dollars for this. And then turn them over to this imposter but due to the circumstances this was never done.

As I advised him that all I could was to make sure that the paper work was completed correctly and advises him if there were any corrections and what they were.

Upon review of an application for seal-ment I discovered that this person had an "Alias Capias" warrant and when I turned in the warrant to the offices with his current address and other personal information the individual never got arrested.

The person who needed his record sealed called the department and said I cleared the record for him in the system. And I supposedly received $ 500.00 bribe for this. This is something I did not have any way of doing, and it was not done by me, if it was done it happed threw the detective who was operating the sting.

Due to the fact that I had filed three different sexual harassment charges against three different offices and an EEOC complaint to get them to back off. They harassed me due to the type of shoes I have to wear; there was this vendetta against me to get me out of the department. They tried every thing the sting is the only thing that worked.

In July of 2001 they arrested me for two counts of illegal use of the department computer for personal use. Everyone knows how much the officers use the computer for personal use but they targeted me. None of them were ever arrested for this just me to shut me up and get rid of the sexual harassment charges.

During this time I had congestive heart failure and wound up in the hospital for one week only to return the next week for the same thing. At this time several test were being performed and that's when the arrested me for the second time, for a hearing I knew nothing about. After the court having been advised by my attorney this part was straightened out and it was not held against me after I had already spent an additional there days in jail. At the time of this hearing I was having a cardiac arthroscopy test done to see if there was a blockage in my heart. The Judge issued an Alias Capias warrant for me and had me arrested and that was the second time.

Bear in mind upon reading the contents of this book that the warrant I told you about in the beginning of this introduction the party has never been arrested for the same thing. The so Called co-defendant the imposter attorney had not been charged and it does not look like he ever will be.

The charges I was facing were for Bribery and Conspiracy when in fact this was just all make up, by the officer who was handling the sting. Take into consideration that typing these applications is not against the law as many paralegal offices do it on a daily basis. So why should they come after me????

Any one has the right to apply for a sealed record in the United States; however this does not mean that it will be automatically granted. I advised the person that the imposter attorney was responsible for the application and the contents therein as well as the party who wants the record sealed.

I have a confession form my so called co-defendant that I was not guilty of what I was supposed to have done and I was set up by the client and the detective. Yet as you will read the outcome of what really transpired.

I could not appeal this because in order to I would have had to admit to something I did not do and would have served a sentence of 16 years. I had to accept a guilty plea to get a withheld adjudication because of my chest pains and other health conditions.

In the Skyburst county there was a Judge who wrote a false police report while drunk saying "She was drugged and raped." This came out that it was false which makes it a felony in this State. She is still on the bench as of the writing of this book. The charges were dropped against her by the state attorney's office who failed to press the charges for felony D U I.

WHERE IS THE JUSTICE IN ALL OFTHIS???????????????

You as the reader would agree that neither I nor You could ever work or be around them ever again. If I had known about the tactics this police department used I would have never joined this or any other department. Wahoo what hind site can give you.!!!!!!!!!!!!!!!!!!!!

As you will read officers ran things in the computers all the time but when I tried to protect myself look at the out come. Remember the complaints those did not help me either.

I am disabled now and can not hold a job because of severe depression and my health. I have an extremely hard time on meeting new people and trusting them, and not being able to see that they will not fuck me over or be able to gain their trust to any kind of level.

IT IS YOUR DECISION THAT YOU WILL FORM UPON YOUR COMPLETION OF THIS BOOK REMEMBER THAT THE PARTIES IN THIS STORY WHICH IS ALL TRUE CARRY A BADGE AND A GUN DO YOU FEEL THERE IS ANY JUSTICE OR THAT YOU ARE PROTECTED. !!!!!!!!!!!!!!!!!!!!!!!!!!!!!!!! !!!!!!!!!!!!!!!!!!!!!!!!!!!!!!!!!!!!!!!!!!!!!!!!!!!!!!!!!!!!!

An Autobiography by Lee-Ann

# CHAPTER ONE

IT WAS IN FALL of 1980, I was waitressing at the family diner, and the sunset was beautiful. I used to always loose myself in the horizon looking through the window. The job was not bad. Actually it paid all my bills, but I always felt like something was missing. The days would go by and the same customers would come in everyday and would make my work easier. Some would tell a few jokes make us laugh. Some would make us cry from laughing so hard. Of course then you had some that were so mean that you just did not want to wait on them for all the money in the world.

I had a call customer come in on a particular day and as she sat in my station she said to me, as she was placing her order "why are you doing this? Do you like working as a waitress? How long have you been doing this? You know you could be a dispatcher for the county, for the fire department and have a retirement fund for when you get older because I'm sure you don't want to be a waitress for the rest of your life or do you?."

I said "well I like my job; it gives me the opportunity to meet all kinds of people. It pays my bills and I'm happy." She said "I think you should try it and if it doesn't work out you could always come back to what you like best." I thought about going to work for the fire department for a while. Why would I want to leave what I liked doing best? I had fun doing this and I really liked my customers. I was young and when you're young you don't always look at it the way other people do so when I went home and spoke to my second parents about this proposal. They told me "that they would stand behind me in any decision I made."

I went to work the next day and spoke to my manager and she said "I could always come back to where I was working if I ever needed a job and understood that I needed to grow in my lives endeavor."

Today is a beautiful day. I am looking out the window and there is a sunset that is breathtaking. It is to pretty to be working. My boss came up to me and asked me "if I like the Beach Boys?" I said "Yes, why?" She said "Well, it's early slow tonight and there is a concert going on at the music theater so here are two tickets why don't you and a friend go the concert?" I said "You're kidding?" I called up my best girlfriend Sue and asked her what she was doing for the night? She replied "Nothing" Why Lee-Ann? So I told her to go get a shower and get ready to go to a show that we were going to see the Beach Boys in concert.

We went and had the best time any two people could have. She said "Okay and we WILL have the best time." The concert was so good. I really like working here. These people are like my family not just co-workers. I guess you can understand that part. We are just a little place but that sometimes makes it like a family.

I am at dinner, when these two girls came in this evening it's about six pm whom I don't really care for. One knew who I was and asked for my station. I asked my co- worker "Lavern to pick up the table because I did not like the party." Lavern said "She was on a call party" In the restaurants you can ask for a certain waitress or waiter and get their station. I said "Darn, I really don't like her, but I guess I have to serve her now. Lavern said "Why don't you like her?" I said "because her car has been outside my boyfriend's house quite often and the lights were off and I'll guarantee you that they were not holding hands on the couch" I said "Oh by the way let me correct myself. Let me say my ex-boyfriend. If you know what I mean."

I went to the table and introduced myself as their waitress and told them I would be right with them. I asked if I could bring them something to drink on my return. As she looked up at me, with this evil look in her eye, she ordered a hot tea. She said "she was ready to order what they wanted and I told them I would be right back to take the rest of their order."

I wasn't overly friendly but I wasn't disrespectful either, because that's not me. I went and got the drinks and desserts and coffee and other foods for other tables as well as for their table. This way I didn't waste time. I always did this anyway so it wasn't something new to me. I couldn't wait for her to leave the restaurant. I gave them the check and asked if they needed anything else? I then went over to my other tables and attended to them.

I had three other desserts to get at the same time so I got them rather than walking back and forth just because it was someone you necessarily wanted to get out of your hair. I put the drinks on a tray and the desserts in my hand and extra plate for them to share the piece of pie with, so when I went to put it down on the table, the pie started to titer totter on the side of the dish and I was really hoping that it would go in her lap for having the nerve to come into the restaurant, and then even having more nerve to sit in my station. "What a witch". I truly wished it would have gone in her lap and that's not me.

I went on to serve my other customers and everybody else got a good laugh at that one. I could not do this again if I tried or practiced this for a scene in a movie. They all wondered why she even came in to the place where I worked. I was cleaning the tables and just as she was walking out to her car, it looked very familiar. That stupid red car that was parked behind my boyfriend's house all night. It just confirmed to me that all along I knew it to be true.

He came into the restaurant that day and sat in my station and I was as cold as ice. He asked "What was wrong?" I told him "You just missed your girlfriend, that drives the red car, that is parked behind your house when you call and ask me to come over and meet you or to go to the movies with you. So maybe you should go see her." He said "What are you talking about" I said "She just had the nerve to come in here and ask for my station. Have a nice day."

When I told him about this and that I realized I've seen this car before he of course tried to deny the fact that she was ever in his house.

I told him not to insult me or think that I was a dummy or something because I could tell him a few stories he would not like about himself that are true.

At the time I was dating someone else. He was not a police officer. I could not believe what I saw. I brought this to his attention and he said "Oh she's only a friend. I let her through one of the guys on the squad." I told him what happened and he said "Why would she ask for my station, does she need to hear what I sound like and do I meet her expectation." Of course no answers were there for any of those questions.

Today is Monday morning and I think I will go down and put my application in for the police department. I have been thinking about it and what do I have to loose if I do get hired. If I don't like it I can always change my career back to being a waitress.

I went down to the personal department of the police department and filed out the application and left it there. About two months later my background investigation was completed. I was contacted and asked "if I was still interested in becoming a dispatcher for the fire department?" I went down for the training, and while in training I had a supervisor who thought the proper way to handle training was to hauler at you. For something you either did not understand or did incorrectly. If you asked for help either on the air or if you asked someone to take over the air because you were confused, with the units on the road hearing and knowing you were in training, they were more cooperative then she was.

They knew what to do and already went to the scene and then when they had to call in for the times for there records they said "they started out and they would have told me that they were in route because they knew that I was new and they did not want me to loose my job." A lot of them knew me and respected me because they knew me from the restaurant . You just don't always click with someone and then it makes it harder on you in the long run I gather so they cannot accept this.

I pulled the headset off my head and asked "To speak to the shift commander and explain to the shift commander and have the tapes pulled." All the units on the road called in and asked "What was going on? and why was this necessary for the supervisor to do this in this situation, why did she not handle it and go over it with me in a more professional manner?" I thought to myself that these people do not know how to train people nor how to talk to people. I understand on the job training, but they should take over the air and let you listen and learn at times. If they didn't like me for some reason I truly wouldn't know why. I was only there for two months.

Well just like you would by now expect I was written up, and this caused a big problem saying "I could not handle the stress of such a job." I replied "I do not take to people hollering at me on the air with all the units in the county hearing this and not having the respect of any of them in the future." This did not set well with me. They then told me "to find another office to transfer to where I could go to in the county." I did not know where to go at this point and I resigned from the fire department not knowing any better.

I had no idea that me time could get transferred over to the police department, because they did not tell you these kinds of things. This is the kind of things they don't want you to know. They would not help you find a job that would let your time transfer over to another department.

Excuse me if I cannot handle stress, what do you think handling two waitressing job's at the same was, I would work from 6:00 in the morning until 3:00 pm and then from 5:00 pm until 11:00pm. That would definitely cause you some stress but I handled this with no problem and I purchased a home full of furniture and a car with these jobs and then I let one go. As far as stress, well I think I did pretty dam well with that.

5

# CHAPTER 2

I APPLIED TO THE County Employee's Credit Union at this time thinking that this was a county job. I will start this job on Monday morning and work as an accounting clerk. I will be checking all accounts that are open and closed in a computerized book to see if they have been closed or if they are currently open and up to date.

As I'm at the diner working some of the guys from the fire department come in. They were talking about what happened today and when I went to take their order one of the Guys said "Excuse me, was that you in training that that happened to this morning on the air?" I said "Yes." They said "That was not right; somebody should have taken over the air and then told you what to do, and let you listen in so that in that instance nobody would have gotten hurt or killed." I said "I truly agree with that but the party training me did not want to take the time to handle it properly instead she wanted to ridicule me."

They sat in my station and we talked more about other options that are available to me and what I could do. I am driving home from work at about midnight from the diner and was going to stop at the grocery store to get some milk. When all of a sudden I heard this awful noise coming from someone's car. I thought boy am I glad that that's not my car.

I had just had an oil change done earlier that day at Zayer's department store in the automotive section. The noise got louder and louder and then all of a sudden there was a big white cloud of smoke under the hood of my car. Then I thought oh my it is my car and is it going to blow up now what do I do?

My mind was not on my car instead it was focused on, "What is I Going to do?" ?????? I said to my self "Transfer to another department. I don't take to people hollering at me like that." Then I wondered if I made a big mistake because I truly was happy here doing what I was doing??????

So I pulled over and shut the car off. I was so scared. It was pitch black.. I called the station where Jon worked to see if he left thinking maybe he could come pick me up. They told me to put a sticker on my car and no one would tow it away , but he was already gone for the night. Did I want them to call him at home? I said "No thank-you I can do that, Thank-you and have a nice night." I tried to call him and he did not answer the phone at home. I thought maybe he did not get home yet or maybe he went to the gym to work out I would try him later.

Before work today when I had the oil change done on my car I thought it can't hurt to be done at a department store while I was shopping. OH my, How I was wrong. Here comes a tow truck, it just happens to be some of my friends. They put the car up on the tow truck and said "Hey sweetie you don't have any oil in the car." I said "What do you mean. I just had an oil change done today." They said "I'll tell you what, so that nothing happens to the car we will tow it to your house and in the morning we will tow it to Toyota.

Call us in the morning when you get up and we'll tow it in the morning. I said "Thank-you Can I give you some money?" They said "Don't insult us." I said "Never, I love you guys." They took me home and I was so furious. I could not sleep. Back then we didn't have rules that you could not go swimming at any hour of the day. I had to get this madness out of me so I went swimming. My neighbors came out and asked what happened, and I told them. They all got there suits on and went

in the pool with me. I lived in a young population apartment. In the morning I got ready and called the guys and we took the car to Toyota.

They put the car up on the racks and told me that there was no oil in the car and that the engine and short block were locked in place. I lost both the engine and short block and back in the 70's it would have to come from Tokyo. I wouldn't have my car for about a month. I was livid. I said "Could you tell me how this happened, when I just had an oil change done yesterday?"

They said "They left both seals on the filter and ruined your engine." I said "Could you call them and help me fight this to make them pay for this because I can't fight them and know I don't have my car." The manager at Toyota did everything he could. He said "How are you going to get around?" "Do you need a rental car?" I said "Yes. I don't have a way home." He said "I'll take care of it. Just sit in my office." I said "I'm afraid if I sit in your office I might fall asleep because I have been awake for 24 hours. I need to get some sleep."

About an hour later, I said to the guy "Where is the person that is bringing this car, is he making this car for it has been a while? Could you check on it, because, I am ready to fall asleep and would not get up for a while?" He said "Don't look now but he is walking down the isle as we speak." I said "Holy Crap, that's my rental agent." He said "Do you know him?" I said "NO, but I wouldn't mind getting to know him." He said "He's single." I said "Really" Nothing else was said on my part.

We got in the car to go the office and I said " I needed to take a nap or I would not be able to drive myself home that I was real tired." I asked him "What his name was?" He said "My name is Bob, and every one calls me that but if you want to call me by another name you can, I would like it, and I think it's cute that you need to take a nap. That's like my little sister." I said "I am no body's littler sister I am fully awake now. Let's get something straight I'm nobody's little sister." "I have five older sisters, and I am fully awake now. Besides I better watch where we are going so I know where the office is to return the vehicle when my rental is up. I have been up for 24 hours and I am really tired." When I got back to the office I filled out the paperwork and thanked him and went home.

Later that day when I woke up their were flowers on my door step saying "I'm sorry I didn't mean to offend you. How about dinner?" You can reach me at, the number, signed Bob." I called and said " Bob, Hi this is Lee-Ann I accept your apology, but only if you let me buy you dinner because that really wasn't me. I was so tired that I was not myself. I am not normally grouchy like that." He said "I can't let you buy dinner but I accept your apology." We went out to dinner and a movie and then said "Goodnight." About a week later he called me again and asked me out to dinner. Needless to say he asked "Me if we could start dating." I said "I would like that." He seemed like a nice enough guy.

This is about an hour later and as I am driving down the road I got stopped by a police officer because my tag on the rental car was expired. The officer told me "that he was going to give me a ticket because I had an expired tag". I told him "that it was a rental car and that I had just picked the car up about an hour ago and I would go the rental car agency in the morning as they are closed now to get the correct tag if he did not write me a ticket. I showed him the rental agreement and I guess I got lucky because it worked." I did not get a ticket and he let me go. I was a little hot under the collar thinking that this was not a large company and that they could keep the cars in line at least with the tags.

I called up Bob and told him that I had a warning from the police and that it was on the rental car. I would bring it in to the office but I had to work. He said "No problem, he would bring the correct tag to my job because it was something that got over looked by the office and it should not have happened." He brought it to me and placed it on the car. How sweet. We started to date at this point. He is really a nice guy.

Today I have an interview with the Credit Union. I am going to take the position working in the County Credit Union. I thought it was a County job. I found out later that it was not a county job. I am very happy working here. I am in this job for about three years. I worked with the loveliest crew. My job was initially to assist the young lady in opening accounts. I was asked to take this book and go through it to check and see if any members had more than one account. If any member had more than one account I had to consolidate them into one.

If a member had three accounts then they were to be consolidated into one and when the last one was closed they could not open any more accounts. Sometimes I would find members that had four or five different accounts and I would bring this to the supervisor's attention. If they had more than the allotted amount of accounts and had loans under these accounts, this would cause a bigger problem. They would have to be consolidated and then closed and then the member would get a letter explaining that they received a loan under false pretense.

Either by neglect of the account technician or just because she wanted to do someone a favor, She was known to do that at times. I understand doing someone a favor and bending the rules here and there, but sometimes there are always exceptions to the rules, but not when you misuse them.

She told me "That I had to close these accounts and send out letters to these members explaining that they had too many accounts and per the rules and regulations of the Credit Union, they were only allowed to have three." This book was approximately fifty pages long and computerized. I would get additional pages that I had to add to it every day. Once I caught the book up it was not hard to keep it up and keep track of the files. The manager and assistant manager of the Credit Union were very impressed with this.

Then the manager and assistant manager called me into the office today and said "We would like to know if you would take over the position of the Opening Accounts Clerk. We are going to let our current one go because she does not do the job correctly and you are very efficient in your job. We would greatly appreciate it if you would take the job."

I told them "I would accept the job with honors, but I really felt bad that someone was losing their job because of me." They said "They were ready to get rid of her because "She would leave the office and not do her job, or I would not have had a book so big to consolidate in the first place." I guess with that they had a point.

But I really did not want to make someone lose there job. I would assist the loan officers in pulling credit reports when I did not have anymore accounts to open for the day. Then I would have to help file the applications in the shelves. Everybody always left at the same time because we did not work in the best area of town. We used to work around the back of the baseball stadium and it was really hard to get to so we all walked together in case anyone got hurt. We were always there for each other.

They manager and supervisor told me that the girl that was doing this job before me, we will call her Else, was not doing the job correctly and they were going to let her go. I would start at this position on Monday morning. I worked this position for three years. I would also assist the front desk answering the phones, filing the loans and pulling the credit reports. I would assist the tellers as needed. I also trained our receptionist on handling the new clientele.

Today is Lila's birthday and we are all getting ready to have an office party for her. She knows nothing about this. We told her that we needed to have someone pick up lunch, because the orders are always screwed up, so we sent her out and when she got back everything was set up. She told us that they said that lunch was delivered to the office by mistake so she just came back and at that time they called us and told us that she was on her way back to the office to let us know when she left the shop. This was all set up as it was catered in and set up that way. She was so surprised. She had such a great time, Lila is so funny and that makes a party in it's self.

Bob went to Colorado to go Skiing on vacation and I had to work so I could not go. He called me up today and asked "Honey why don't you come over for dinner tonight? I missed you." I said Bob "You were not suppose to be home for another week, what happened? Don't tell me that you broke a bone or something, or I'll laugh my butt off at you." I was just teasing him. He said "No, I really miss you." I said "That's sweet." I would love to come to dinner. What time would you like to go?" We went around 7:00 pm.

I took my shower and put on this little sun dress and matching shoes and stockings. I would dress like this with sun shoes and stockings to match. I wanted to surprise him. When I got to the house I did not know where we were going or if I was dressed appropriately but I figured we could go to dinner accordingly to what I was dressed for. He thought that was so sweet.

When I got up to his house, I couldn't help it when I got in the door, there he was sitting in the living room with a broken arm. He fell off the ski sloop. I started laughing. I said "I'm so sorry, but I really can't help it. I knew something was wrong and you wouldn't tell me. Sweetheart. How can I make it all better? Should I kiss it and make it all better?" He had a stick shift car at the time and it was not easy for him to drive at the time, so he really had a hard time getting around town. His dad traded cars with him for work, and we used my car to go out. Poor Baby!!!!!!!! We did not exchange gifts at Christmas time. We did not spend Christmas together this year.

I told my co-worker that I was going to go to the county personal and apply for a secretarial job with the county so that I would have retirement benefits. I wanted to see if I could apply for the Police Department. She told me that she thought that it was a good thing that I was going to do this. She said "that she was excited for me that I wanted to go work for the police department and fully understood."

She was a loan officer and backed me up all the way in my decision to go and put my application in. She told me to call that morning and say I was having car trouble of some sort and I was on my way and she would back me up. So I called in that I had a flat tire and was waiting for someone to help me as they knew that I have trouble with my hands and can't even attempt to change a tire.

Today is a sunny day. I'm so nervous. I have my interview with the Police Department. I hope I don't mess it up. I am going to go in very calm and collective. I will let them start the interview and see how it goes. I will not overpower the interview. I work with computers before so that should be a good thing. I hope I do well. I'm so nervous.

I made a direct referral interview with the Police Department. Upon setting up the appointment with the records section, the secretary called and wanted to know if I could change the interview with the Commander that I had scheduled? I had to tell her "No, I had to take the day off to set this interview up, and I could not afford to take another day off, so it had to be that day." When I went in for my interview, Mr. Learn told me that he liked the fact that I was very forceful in getting my interview that day, because he knew I would be the right person for the job."

During my interview I was very calm and collective. Not too forceful. I answered all the questions, and he showed me all around. Then I didn't hear from him for about two months. I thought darn I was too forceful in my interview. Next time I won't be so strong.

Now as I am making dinner I get a phone call asking me "If I can come down to the investigations sections so that they can ask some questions as part of their interview process and investigation?" This was routine in their hiring process, so I asked them "what time did I have to be there because I was making dinner?" They said "How about 6:00pm, is that convenient for you?" I said "Okay, but may I ask what this is about? I haven't done anything and I would appreciate knowing why I am being questioned by the Police?" They said "Didn't you place an application for employment with us about two months ago?" I said "Yes." Then this part of our routine background investigations." I said "Okay. I'll be there. Please give me the address." I went down and answered all the questions as needed. I told my girlfriend that I applied and asked her if I could use her as a personal reference. She said "of course you can and I will give you a great reference."

Sue and I were best friends since seventh grade. We used to hang out at either her house or mine. I have five sisters and she has a brother and a sister. Her house was mine and mine was hers. We shared everything from clothes to sisters to brothers to parents. My mom used to love it. We would always go swimming at my house and have pool parties at my house because we had a pool and a lake behind the house. My mom was considered the neighborhood mom.

She would do anything for you. If she didn't feel good we went to someone else's house or stayed at mine and just kept an eye on her and did our home work keeping an extra eye on her. She was so sick with cancer. No one ever let on to her that we were watching her we just said "It was a study hall in my room but we would be quite, and if she needed something to let me know. I would do the house work in between and let her sleep."

It was our senior year and I was working in a Garden Center at a Company called Woolco. I would walk into the store with my mom and the main cashier would call me to my register thinking that I was on duty. I would pick up the phone and tell her that I was shopping with my mom. She would ask "If I could work because they were short handed." I would turn around and ask "My mom if she minded because it was time with my mom and I wanted to spend it with her. I would have to have her come and pick me up if she didn't mind." She said "She didn't care.

So I worked at the register. Then my mom or my boyfriend would pick me up. We went to get up for church this one Sunday morning and I could not stand up. I had these terrible bumps all over my legs. I looked like I had the measles all over. My legs hurt so badly. I called my mom in my room and showed her my legs. I told her "That they hurt so bad that I could not stand up and she went and got my father. He picked me up and they took me to the Hospital. I saw a Dermatologist and he asked "If I was near any Bats." I said "No, There are no bats in MY STATE.

He told me that actually there were bats in this state and they could have bitten me and that they would have left this kind of mark on my leg." I then replied that I was working in a garden center in a Department store with fertilizer and yard chemicals." He tested me for different chemicals in the fertilizer and found out that I am allergic to Sulfa. I had to leave the garden center and work the main cash registers of the store. That was NO PROBLEM for me.

During the holidays, they would always put me on the express lane for some reason. It was so busy. I was always busy. This helped make the time fly by before you knew it the day was over. They made sure I got my holiday shopping done. Even if it was after hours because I always came in for them. My girlfriend Sue would come up and we would be shopping and they would ask "If I would take a register?" Sometimes

I would say "Not today, I'm shopping for Mom, she's not feeling well today, and I have to get back home." They understood.

This is how long I have known Sue and just a few of the things that Sue and I would do together. By the way this is just one of my girlfriends whose name is Sue. Her middle name is Ann.

Sue and I would go shopping then she would always want to go for a hot fudge sundae at Howard Johnsons. She used to love having a mint chocolate chip ice cream with hot fudge topping over a brownie topped with whip cream. That was her favorite.

Now as two months have passed I received that call while at the Credit Union and asked "If I was still interested in coming to work for the Police Department?" I said "Yes, I am however, I would like to give my current boss a two weeks notice." He said "I would appreciate the same respect from you, I will expect to see you in two weeks at 06:00 hrs, and welcome aboard." I said "Thank you see you then."

I still worked my part time job as a waitress so I could buy my first house. I wanted to save as much as I could so as to have a good amount down. I wanted to purchase what ever I needed for my house without putting it on credit cards. I was very pleased with that. It made it all worth while working the two jobs. I told my job that I applied to work at the police department and they said "I know, they were here for a background check on you already. Everything is okay. Don't worry. We took care of you." I said "I would still like to work part time so that I can save for my house and put it all together. I am still working on my goal." They said "It was okay, I was welcome to do that as long as I wanted."

After three great years at the Credit Union, I am leaving there. I sat down and typed a letter of resignation for her with a two weeks notice with it. I asked "Her if I could talk to her about something?" I said Marty I received a call from the Police Department and they said "If I was still interested in coming to work for them that I could start in two weeks." I told her "That I love working for her, however I have always wanted to work for the Police Department and if it didn't work out could I possibly come back."

She wrote me back a letter of acceptance of my resignation and told me "that I could come back anytime I needed a job. That my work was above satisfactory and she was very proud to have me as a worker." She said "I knew about it because they were here for a background check on you as an employee and a personal check. We gave you a great reference and are very sorry to see you go."

I left and went to work that night and I was a little at edge. I wasn't sure if I made the right decision or not. I really liked my position at the Credit Union and I didn't mind working at the diner. It gave me a chance to meet people and have a little extra cash. What's the harm? I had benefits with the Credit Union; however, it was not like the Police Department. All the people that I worked with are wonderful and we were like a little family so why didn't I just stay? I could have worked at the diner if I needed to for extra cash or at my sister's store and still had a retirement plan just a little different one.

# CHAPTER 3
# 1983

TODAY IS MONDAY MORNING and it is six o'clock in the morning. I am to report to the job at the station. I am a little nervous. I am going to work with a bunch of new people and this is all new to me. Like any one else you would be a little on edge. I am wearing a red dress, black shoes, and stockings. My hair is long and wavy. I did not bring anything for lunch today so I will have to find something to get to eat around here. I guess the girls will tell me where there is a coffee shop for lunch. I know that there are new people in every job you go to but for some reason this one was just a little bit different.

I started out as a clerk typist II working in the bond hearing unit. I would have to get files pulled for the court and make copies for the court, sign them out and re-file the files back in the shelves. I would file papers sent in from the State Department of Law Enforcement that had to go into the files and match the files and numbers and names to make sure there is not more than one of those files. I would have to file papers from the FBI in the files and re-file the files. These two papers are from different agencies so there were different amounts. Sometimes I would receive three times the amount from the SDLE than the FBI. I would have to make copies and get them ready for the courts. Then take them over to the courts. This had to be done on a timely manner.

After I was introduced into my duties for the day it was lunch time, they took me to the hospital across the street to Harde to show me where the coffee shop was. This came in very handy as when we did

17

not have any lunch with us we just went there. Sometimes we would order Chinese or pizza but most of the time we went and had a salad. We were all on diets half the time anyway. This is very typical of any office for most of the employees are trying to be skinner than the other one. We would sometimes eat popcorn and a bottle of grapefruit juice, and drink water. Sometimes I would bring in fresh picked grapefruits from the trees in the backyard because we had so many and we would eat those for lunch for our diets. We never had to worry about buying them because of the trees in my back yard.

I am filling rap sheets in the jackets and I have filed about six hundred of these in one day. I have to pull the rap sheet, number them, put them in numerical order, pull the jackets, file the papers in the jackets then file the jackets back on the shelves. While doing this I would find misfiled jackets so I would just pull them and put them where they belonged.

Some of my other duties besides filing papers were to go through the jackets and clean them out. I would have to make sure that they were in order and keep them as neatly as possible. I was to get paperwork ready for microfilming. Cleaning the jackets of all staples and putting papers in order. Make sure that there was no person's information that did not belong to that particular jacket. Make sure that all paperwork was in chronological order and final before sending it down to microfilm. I would also have to file something called a Rap Sheet. A rap sheet is the criminal history of an individual. Sometimes you would get boxes and boxes and boxes of these from the Capital Department of Law Enforcement.

It could literally be in the thousands. That would be after pulling them apart so that they matched to the same person. Putting the jacket number on the bottom so it was easier to file and then putting them in chronological order. Then you pull the jacket and check to see if there wasn't already a current one in the file. Sometimes an outdated one would come in before you would get the new one.

So you would have to place the most current one in the jacket that had all the information on it and then shred all the old papers. My supervisor and co-workers in my unit were very nice to work with.

I had three other girls to work with. While filing my files back in the shelves, I would find misfiled jackets which was sometimes very easy to do when you are in a hurry to get them back in the shelves or if they stick together when filling them. So I would place them in the proper places as they are color coated like the ones in the doctors and dentist offices when filled. These jackets are very thick and full. Some are small, some have two, or three volumes to one person. These people are always in trouble and cannot stay out of jail. They are called repeat offenders.

I am pulling files, and very busy now I have this feeling that someone is watching me. I look up and for sure I was right this lady was watching me. I said "Kris can I help you with something?" And her reply was "No". Now when I finished what I was doing I just happened to mention it to my supervisor and asked "If she might have asked her if she needed something or if she knew what that was all about." She said "She would ask her what it was about." Kris could not give her any reason for committing this nonsense. My supervisor said "There was nothing to this. Maybe she was impressed with your work," so I thought nothing of it, and went on about my business.

I am leaving the department for the day and headed home. I am at home and I am watching T.V. When all of a sudden I herd this awful noise out side of my window. I go outside to see what is happening and there is this guy jumping up and down screaming and talking very loud and carrying on like a fool. I'm thinking what this nonsense is. Then my landlord comes downstairs and tells me that it's nothing to worry abut, it's only her son and he won't hurt you. She introduced me to him and that was all it took.

The next time he was outside I asked him "Tommy would you like a glass of water or something to drink?" He said "Okay, that would be nice." He didn't always have control of his faculties because he took a trip on LSD and never came off it. Low and behold if someone where to come up and try and hurt his mom, sister, me or the girl that lived in front of us he would fight you like you would not believe. He knew right from wrong in that instance, and he was good about that.

A few months would pass and all of a sudden, I would be in the files pulling them getting them ready to file paper work and again there is Kris standing there starring at me watching me in the files, as if I'm doing something I'm not suppose to, so I went back to my supervisor.

Again I asked her "If there was a problem again with me being in the files, because of her staring at me. She said she would speak to her and find out what the problem was." During the interview with the supervisor she asked "me to think of her as my mother" my reply was with so much hostility and replied "I already have one and she is not my mother, my mother is in the hospital across the street dying from cancer and I wish that you would stop this nonsense". My unit supervisor then replied, "Lee Ann I'm so sorry I had no idea that your mother was sick, please keep us informed on her condition and if we can do anything for you".

My supervisor said that if my mom should expire it was necessary for funeral leave and I would have to let them know and keep them informed. I asked for them to keep Kris away from me. I asked if I could be excused and return to my job. Needless to say that the meeting did not last long and the bull did not stop. During my life I always worked two jobs including the time during the police department.

I would go to my second job which was still a waitress job and I worked there four nights a week trying to save to get my house. This nonsense kept going on and it was getting on my nerves so I started writing all of this down in a little black book.

There's a girl in the office who's name is Ashley. She ran a tag for someone. I do not know who she ran the tag for. A few days later a couple of Homicide Detectives come upstairs and took her down stairs. They asked her "Who she ran the tag for? Why she ran the tag? Did she know that the car she ran the tag on was found on the side of I 95 shot up with bullet holes, and two people where found dead in the trunk of the vehicle?" She had no idea, and I'm not sure why she really ran the tag or who she ran it for. She was relived of duty and we never heard anything about her again.

I am filling papers and there are detectives at the counter asking for records that they need to be pulled. One piece of paper that needed to be pulled in particular was of the utmost importance, and could not be found, the detective asked me to find it and I naturally would have just taken the paper and start looking except Kris snatched it out of my hands telling me "that it was her unit and I was not part of her unit so I did not need to look for the paper." Now really, if I can find paperwork or misfiled jackets where is the harm in me finding this piece of paperwork that is needed for the detective?

The detective saw what had happened and requested to speak to the unit supervisor to see if this could get resolved. The unit supervisor called me into the office and asked me "Since I was so good at finding misfiled paperwork and jackets, and as it did not matter what it took to find it the paperwork that was needed, the fact that I could find miss filed paperwork was enough. And as it was needed for court right away and because I was fast as I was and it was needed right now she told me to go find it for court."

When I started to look for the paperwork, I started by looking from the beginning where the paperwork is first filed. The first step is the jail booking. Then you have all the rest of the paperwork to sort out. When I started to look through the jail cards. I did this by first cross referencing the names and jail numbers in that pile. I found the correct jail card which is what the Detective needed for court.

Nobody could find it because they were not looking for all the signs, the a.k.a. names, and the jail numbers, as well as the date of arrest and co defendants. When I found this it was for some reason only approximately five jail cards down in a very large file of cards to be filed on the desk of the person who is responsible to file these jail cards. I couldn't believe it because this individual was not that way. She was a nice person, just slow. I gave it to my supervisor, who was extremely surprised at how fast I found the paperwork. She asked me "Where did you find this paperwork, and how did you find it so fast?" I showed her where and "How?" I said "I just cross referenced everything all the information that you gave me and a little more."

I told her I would find it and I would have to start from scratch and to advise Kris that I would have to go into her unit and to stay out of my way so I could find this paperwork. For some reason it did not take long for me to find, fortunately I gave it to my supervisor. She was very grateful as was the officer.

When I went to work at my part time job that particular day, my boss came up to me and asked me "who was this lady with the white hair sitting in the restaurant and why was she asking questions about my performance on my job?" I said, "She was a supervisor at the department, and I don't know why she was asking questions on my job but you don't need to answer any of them."

I asked my supervisor "What station I was on that night," as this was the normal routine to do when you came in the restaurant. You check your station and check to see what kind of side work you would have to do, later so you knew what time frame you had to start doing your side work. As your waitress work it is not only just talking to customers and taking orders, it also means that you have to restock the stations and do prep work. You may have to make certain foods, or roll silverware for the next shift. You have to stock up for the next shift as well. You don't just get tips off the table and walk out the door. Oh some people think it's that easy, but its not.

It doesn't matter what restaurant you work in you have to stock and prepare food for the next shift so that they can serve the customers that come in after you. You can make it look so easy or you can make it look so hard depending how much you really like the job. When I first met Bob I was a waitress and I loved my job. I worked as a waitress for two different companies. Then I went to the Police Department. I still worked in restaurants for a long time. You have to enjoy them or it is not for you.

I was coming to work one morning and the city officers had done a prostitution sting. They picked up a few of these individuals and at six in the morning and they were saying some conversations that are not necessarily conversations you may want to hear. Well, walking into work, they just happen to be transvestites and were talking in the language of the streets. The officers came out of the hallway and told them to straighten up or they could get extra charges placed on them. They straighten up and didn't say any more to me.

The next week at work in the department, I was doing my job getting files, files from down the hall in the microfilm room in order to copy them, and Kris was following me down the hall saying "She was concerned for my safety." As far as I checked my mother taught me how to walk when I was a little girl and she didn't need to be concerned for my safety. Further more I am a big girl and if something were to happen to me in a Police Station I think that there would be enough cops around to take care of the situation.

Why would it be Kris's concern? I would tell my supervisor and ask her to again have her stop this nonsense and she just would not let up. I really don't know what this woman's problem is but I am really getting sick and tired of it. It is just child play. I would tell Bob and he would say "really honey is it really that bad?" because he really did not understand what was going on, when you have someone following you it can cause you to make mistakes and then you get written up and this can causes trouble for you. And a black mark in your personal file and this is very damming to your record cause, when you go to get a promotion it can harm you.

I would go across the hall to the identification room and she would follow to see if I was playing around or getting paper work. When I was trying to see if they had all the paper work I needed so I could get it prepared for court. The identification clerks would ask "what is her problem? Why does she follow you everywhere you go?" I said "I don't know but it truly is getting out of hand."

We are at the diner and it is really busy. We have lines out the door and around the corner. We have a fish and clam fry night all you can eat. We have regular customers that come in for this on every Wednesday and Friday for this dish. Our waiting list is two hours long. We have not had any one complaining yet. Howard Johnson's was very famous for there twenty seven different flavors of ice cream. We would make all different types of dishes with these. We would make mountains, and floats, banana splits and boats. Everybody always helped everybody. We all got along really great again it was like a second family. Why is this lady so intent on following me around?

It was on a Wednesday night and I was working at the restaurant and I was told that I had a party of five on a round table, {common restaurant talk}, so I said, ok, I'll be right there, let me get them some water, and acknowledge them. I had a tray full of drinks and dishes in my other hand when I went to the table, it just happen to be my commander and chief, they are the department heads they did not know it was me until the next day. I brought them their food within seconds, as it was an all you can eat night without them even asking for a second round.

That was the way I always handled any and all of my clients not just the all you can eat parties at any dinner specials on Wednesday and Friday nights. Then I asked "If anyone wanted anymore fish or deserts or could I get them anything else?" I gave them the same courteous service I give all my customers.

The next day in the hall the commander asked the chief "if he knew who I was, and when he said, "No" The commander said, "She is the girl that does the bond hearings and she was our waitress last nigh at dinner. So the Chief said "Thank you for a job well done on both jobs young lady." I said "You are quite welcome."

The Chief said "May I ask you a question?" I said "Sure." He said "How do you get all that hair in that little ball in the back of your head last night?" I said "With a lot of bobby pins." We all laughed and I said "I must get going before my babysitter comes looking for me and went on my way to do my job."

When I got in to work my unit supervisor came up to me and said "Lee-Ann, when you have a minute, can I see you?" I thought oh no, what did I do now? Because of being followed all the time I wasn't sure what the problem was, so I said "Sure when I finished with my court papers. So upon completing my work I went into her office and asked her what was wrong? She said "Nothing was wrong, I have a Jacket that is missing and no one can find it, you seem to be our office detective for finding misfiled jackets and paperwork so whenever you can find it, I would appreciate it." Well I looked for it for a few minutes but to no avail I looked through the transposing numbers and looked for misfiled colors in the sequence.

Unfortunately it was not there. Then I started turning the numbers around in the series to see if the jacket was misfiled that way and that did not work. Then I decided to run it and see if it was maybe with a co-defendants file, or maybe with a double volume jacket series, or just may be by chance it could be misfiled under another name not picked up and in the identification to be consolidated into one jacket. Well no such luck there either.

Well okay, its time to go home, so lets go home for the day and on the way home I'm thinking. This jacket is filed on the end of the cabinet and maybe it fell between the side and shelves. I'll check in the morning. First thing in the morning when I got in the office, I checked for the jacket where it should be filed and followed it straight down to the floor and there it was. I placed it on the supervisor's desk with a note saying "This is the jacket you were looking for" with a smiling face sticky attached to it. Then signed it and went on to do my business. When I got back from court, she asked me to show her where I found it. When I did, she said "No-one would have ever had found it unless we moved because no-one ever thought to look for things there. Thank-you under her breathe my little file detective. I said "You are welcome." I just chuckled and went on to do my work.

# CHAPTER 4
# 1986

TODAY IS A SATURDAY and I am at work today and I am ready to take my paperwork over to the court, oh no! What am I going to do, my shoes broke, and I don't have another pair. You can not go into court without shoes on no matter what. Well I called my mother (my real mom) who lived down by Metro- Zoo to see if she could bring me a pair of shoes and have lunch with me. I would give them right back to her after lunch. Big problem, back then we did not have cell phones, and she was not home. I had to call my second mom and see if she could go into my apartment to get me a second pair of shoes and bring them to me.

As I previously explained I lived in a garage apartment under her and she had a key in case of emergency, and this was a real emergency if ever there was one. However, by the time they got the shoes to me I would have been late to court. Now, I can get my paper work to court and ask the court officer if the Judge would excuse my attire because my shoes broke, or go in shoeless and in stockings?

One of the girls in my office had a pair of slippers. She told me I could use them, but she did not tell me what kind they were at first. They just happen to be a pair of snoopy slippers. I wore them over to the court house and then asked the Court officer to ask the Judge which he would prefer me to do? Wear a pair of snoopy slippers or go barefooted. He said he needed a lift. He then let me in to court. I walked in with snoopy slippers on and presented my paperwork excused myself, and promised it would never happen again and left. I was so embarrassed.

He said "Thank-you I needed that. No problem. Have a good day." Of course that did not go over well with Kris.

However I left a message for my immediate supervisor. The next day I went to Court and I went to the Judge and asked "Him, Your Honor would you write my supervisor a note that you excused my appearance in court yesterday. The issue would cover my shoes and what had happened as I had no other way of getting a pair of shoes" Believe me your Honor I truly sis try. His reply was "You are always on time and I have never had a problem with your work or appearance in my court room. Why Yes I will be glad to write a note for you or I will call your supervisor and explain what happened." He then asked "Who is giving my court this grief"?

I am at my sister's house and my boyfriend calls me up and asked me to meet me him at his house after work. He worked on the same squad as my brother in law and at the same station, so when they got off work I would be with my sister. We were playing a game on him and she was pretending to be me. He could not tell which one of us he was talking to. It was so funny, and my brother in law sat there laughing at him. Then he finally said "May I speak to Lee-Ann please?" Then he said "Would you meet me at my house so we can go out after I get off work today?

I said "Sure, sorry about the joke. We were just having a little fun." When I got there, I could not believe that the red car was parked out side of his house and he would not answer his door. I called his house and he would not answer his phone either. I went back to my sister's house for a while and then went home. He called me the next day as if nothing had happened and I would not answer his call.

We had to go to wellness classes as requirement for working in the department. I went with the girls and we were doing these stair type exercises. We would have to step up and down on this bench for about fifty times or as many times as you can. Some of the girls could not make it. I did it for about fifty times and did not get dizzy, but they were. Then we would go into this aroma therapy class. This would literally take my breath away. I had to step out of the class and have fire rescue come because I could not breathe from the different fumes in the room. I could not explain that as I have never been allergic to anything that I knew of in the past. The rest of the wellness classes so they told me that the next time they had these going on they would exclude me from that part of them and I could go to the rest. I said "Okay, because I enjoyed doing them. I just couldn't handle the fumes."

When filling Rap Sheets I had a jacket on one person who was deceased. I was in the process of putting the file for placement in this section. When filling this rap sheet I noticed something was wrong. On the last two arrests, the second to the last was the deceases date of demise and the last was an arrest. This can not be that way. The last thing on the jacket rap sheet should be the demise information and with this not being so I brought it to my supervisors attention.

I had to bring this information to the identification section so they could double check everything and send it to the State Department of Law Enforcement and return the correct rap sheet to me in order to process the jacket as deceased properly. Once this was done the jacket was prepared for microfilming and placed in the deceased files.

I met a new friend today her name is Rose-Ann. She works the afternoon shift. I work the morning shift. She works the counter. Her job was to get what the officers and detective paperwork Rose-Ann, Tara and I became very close friends and would hang out together. We would take our lunch break together when we worked overtime so that we could see what was new. Then sometimes Rose-Ann's mom would bring lunch up to us and we would pay her for bringing us lunch. We were very close friends. Then all of a sudden Kris would start watching us and say we were not doing our jobs. We were on our lunch breaks and eating. We just ate in the corner so we could eat together.

My supervisor (Whose name is Ana) came up to me and told me that was a good catch Lee-Ann. When the rap sheet comes back to the Identification Section and then it will be given to me. It will then be given to you to finish the jacket. I was diagnosed with Rheumatoid Arthritis. When I was around 16, I was told by a Chiropractor that I would have Arthritis and he could not tell me when it would hit me or how hard it would effect me or if my whole body would be effected. It has started to affect me now. My hands get very sore and start to swell. My knees are sore as well. I am seeing a specialist for this and this is not easy.

They tell me that I should not be doing all the walking that I do and I told them that I do a part time waitress job. He told me that my legs won't take this very much longer. I asked him if walking on the beach in the sand would be good therapy because sometimes walking in the sand makes the muscles in your legs strengthen better. When you have such an illness that is not always the case, you can do more harm than good. He said "I could walk on the beach on the sidewalk to get the ocean sights but not to walk in the sand because it would do more harm." I am suffering from the artists in my shoulders as well. I am truly having a very bad battle with this disease.

When I got to work today, one of my friends, Dee, came up to me and said "Lee-Ann before you go inside I need to tell you something. On the way coming home from the Keys last night Brenda and her daughter were killed in a car accident. We don't know all the particulars on the accident." Dee didn't want me to read this from a poster on the wall when I walked in the office because Brenda and I were very close.

I have quite a few close friends Dee, Lee, Ann, Libia, Tara, Rana, Iarey, John, Ana, Tifinay, and Besty. On Saturday mornings after we did our bond hearings we would make breakfast. Well one Saturday morning the girls wanted waffles, they told me I did not know how to make waffles. I brought the ingredients to make them from scratch and made them. Because I was a white girl I couldn't cook from scratch. I told them I came from a family of farmer's and could make them waffles and probably a few other dishes. They never told me I didn't know how to cook again.

We would have luncheons at least ounce a month just to have a little get together so that everyone can be with each other and know that we all stilled cared for each other. We always made sure that there was plenty left over in case the guys came up or over from the other offices, they usually did and gave us money for the dishes so we used it for the paper products. Then we made sure there was plenty of that in stock.

We all made a covered dish and brought it in so that no one had to bring in all the expensive things. We always had extra paper products from the last covered dishes so we didn't need to get more. Then the guys from Homicide got wind of this and they wanted to join in and so we let them. They were on the second floor. Then the guards at the front desk joined in too. It was very nice.

Well today the computers were going on the blink and wouldn't stop. We had to call the computer room and they kept telling me what to do. One person in particular I became friends with and when we had to call he would ask for me to get on the phone so we could get the computers working. He occasionally would come by the office and take me out for dinner just as friends. Today is my Birthday and he called me up and asked "If I had any dinner Plans?" I said "No." He said "Okay, may I take you out to dinner?" I said "Okay." I didn't think anything of it and when he came to pick me up, he brought me a small gift as well. "How very sweet of him." I said to him " I never told you when my Birthday was, how did you find out, did one of the girls tell you?" He said "No I have my ways."

Well when we got back in to the office, one of the girls, named Kama, did not like the fact that he took me out to dinner for my Birthday. She was extremely jealous of the fact that we went out to dinner together and that he was talking to me. He was a friend and co-worker. We would go out to a movie or for a cup of coffee so we could talk about things that would go on in the office.

He knew what would happen because when he had to come into the office to fix the computers he would see how these women would back stab you and try and be your friend while someone was there. If he called up to have the computers fixed by phone he would always ask for me because he did not want to bother with any of the other girls as they did not want to try to deal with the wires saying this was not part of there job description. So as I did not have a problem with that it was usually for me who got the computers back on track with his advice and instructions.

I had an interview for a part time job today, and I bet you will never guess where it is. Believe it or not, it is for the Playboy club, to sing. Yes, that's right. I love to sing, and I applied. So I put my application in for outside approval as I did for any other part time job for the department to singing at the club and to my surprise, it was denied. Just for singing. I couldn't understand this. I asked why. They said "It wasn't for singing it was the location and my choice of the kind of part time job."

Now when I am looking back after all the shit that has been pulled upon me, you will see, I often wonder if my decision was right. I still love to sing, and it takes my stress away. As we learn to say, and if I may take someone else saying "If I can turn back time?" Dear Lord Help Me!!!!!!!!!!!! My interview and audition was to Roberta Flacks "The First Time If Ever I Saw Your Face." If I would have had my choice any other place to have a singing interview I'm sure I could have kept up with singing. It is funny how things turn out, I have been around other people of influence that think that I can sing at this point in my life and think that I missed my calling. As I sing when I make them subs on a sub line in a sub shop now.

You always look for ways to better yourself and in ways in which you may enjoy yourself. I love singing. If any of us can really see the future as to what would happen, I'm sure my decision to do something different would have been made.

Today we had a Blood Drive at the Station. Everybody was joining in so I decided I would do it with them. Let me tell you, when the nurse put that needle in my arm she went into the vein and did it wrong, she literally caused a huge bruise on my arm me. I was black and blue so bad that my arm hurt like the dickens. The head nurse asked if she could try the other arm. I was really reluctant but didn't want to seem like a baby, so I let her try. She hit it the same way. The next day, both of my arms were literally purple, and I could not move them, they hurt so much. I went to my doctor to have them checked and he was livid.

He called the company because he was concerned with the possibility of blood clots, and had them monitor my arms until they were normal again so they watched me that I did not get blood clots or that one did not break and travel and something else worst happen. I was supposed to have a blood test taken, and I could not go through with it. I wonder why? It took two weeks for my arms to heal.

Well this is a Saturday, and after coming back from bringing papers to the court I went into the ladies room to refresh myself and then I was going to start working on two and three volume jackets reducing them and getting them ready for microfilming. You have to separate the pages and make sure the pages are in order and place them in chronological order and make sure there are no staples and paper clips in the way for filming. I just went across the hall, to go to the bathroom, I don't think Kris needed to be concerned for me or my safety but really I don't think the commode is going to swallow me .

She decided to come into the bathroom to tell me that she put a double volume jacket on my desk, and that she wanted to check up on me. I just flushed the commode I was so mad. There was a co-worker in the vanity of the lavatory, and she could not believe what she heard or saw. My co-worker said to me "I cannot believe she just did that, if I were you I would tell another supervisor so someone knows what is going on. What is this woman's problem?"

I told her I thought my mother did a good job on potty training me and that I was not afraid of the commode. I told her that I was going to refresh my face and then go to the identification section to see if there were any more papers I needed to work on before going back to my desk, so I did not have to see this supervisor. I wrote my supervisor a note about what happened and told her that I wanted to speak to her, and it was of the utmost importance and emergency that she "Call me in the morning when she came in, because I was so livid about the situation and I wanted it to stop." She called me and she said "That when I came in the next morning we would have a meeting with the head supervisor so we could talk about what was going on.

Her question to me was "Would this be satisfactory to me?" I told her "I would speak to her in the morning." I was not sure what to expect or what would really be done about it as I know these two ladies went to lunch together often. What did I think would have really been done about it?

During this time, my mother was extremely sick and was diagnosed with breast cancer again and this time we were told they could not get her in remission. She went through hell. Mom I surely miss you. I still lived under this couples home in that small garage apartment and I called them my second mom and dad. This was an extremely hard time to call them this. I told them what was happening at the time. Of course they were there for me and there daughters and the people that lived in the front house were also there. We were like our own little family. We did everything together. We used to go shopping together. Take walks together.

To go get the Sunday paper on Saturday night together so we could look at the coupons together and cut coupons and laugh at some of the dumb ones. Mom and Dad Pen I miss you. They knew of the nonsense that was going on. The young guy, his name was Jose was a mechanic and working in a small garage, so I told him, "Why don't you go to the county and get a job as a mechanic for the county." That way you have benefits and with the kids and Cheryl, his wife, at least he would have security that way."

Well he did, and by chance he just happened to get a mechanics job at the station that I worked at. Jose was very well liked. They were there for me through all this abuse. We did all kinds of things together. We became best friends. When I bought my first house, they came over and we had a little house warming party. We would always be together on the weekends either at her house or mine and through the birth of both of their girls.

When I came out of the lavatory I spoke to another supervisor and advised her of what had transpired. I asked if this was necessary and she told me "no." I went back to my desk and wrote it down in my little black book. I was off on Sunday and Monday so when I came back on

Tuesday I told my supervisor and I asked to speak to the unit supervisor. The unit supervisor asked me to have a meeting with her and Kris in her office and that it is today this morning, and we did have the meeting, and Mrs. Coed said "Why don't you think of her as your mother?"

I said I have already told you "I have my mom and she is in the hospital across the street with cancer and is extremely sick. Thank you very much. Please excuse me." Mrs. Coed later came up to me and said "I'm sorry Lee-Ann I didn't know and if there is anything we can do let us know." I did remember you telling us this. Please keep me informed on the status of your mom.

Now as you are allowed to take tests to better yourself and get promotions which at this time I had signed up to do so. And as you would be I was getting tired of this nonsense. Now as I had to have surgery done, and my doctor did not know if it was cancerous or not and I was very concerned with the outcome as my mother was very ill and near death at this time from cancer it was hard for me. They had to do a laparoscope because I kept on having severe pelvic pain.

They could not find out what was causing it, and it was not as advanced as it is today. I was hemorrhaging like I was having a baby and there was no explanation. My doctor gave me medication to try and stop this, but could not explain it. It had severe pain and a huge bleeding problem. As you can see I had a lot of things on my mind. Why would I write stupid letters to the chief or want some dumb lady on my back that I did not work for?

While all this was going on I came up with an Idea that would save Detectives, Officers, & Record clerks, time when looking at microfilm, while looking for certain information that was more important and which would save them a lot of time in investigations and court. My supervisor gave me a commendation on this "Saying that this could save the county and officers a lot of money." Kris would not stop her nonsense, so at this point I requested a meeting with the chief of police.

Upon having the meeting I said to him "I have a problem with a supervisor". I had a book of dated material of what she had done with me. His reply was "Let me guess, it's Kris." "I said "Yes, and I will not stand for any more of her following me around everywhere I go." His reply was "It will be taken care of." I placed this information on his desk and apologized for the way it was written and not typed. I told him if I had to type it I would become madder by the minute because I had to rewrite it, and I kept getting more upset by the minute so if I had to rewrite it I can't do that. I advised him if she did not stop I would take it higher until she left me alone.

I never did anything to this woman and I have no idea what her beef with me was all about. I had taken a test to get a promotion that I applied for previously. I went to afternoons, and to a different department. I was in the same building but a different department. She was told to leave me alone.

Do you remember me telling you of the red car behind the police mans house earlier well, guess what its back behind his house today? I called him on the phone and he would not answer the phone. We had planed to have a date today and I left my sisters house to go on this date. I called my sister and asked her "Trudy, not the one that had the baby, could I come by and talk to you?" She said "Sure, but I thought you and Jon had a date?"

When I got to the house, we were talking and I said "I thought so to, but somebody else is parked behind his house and he will not answer the phone." I never want to talk to him again. I'm not a door mat for him. She asked me "What are you going to do?" I said "I don't know but I think that is really low." I didn't call him and when he called me like nothing ever happened he asked "Why haven't you called?" I said ""Why should I, I'm sure the slut you have over with the red car is doing just fine. Until you can guarantee me that you are safe, I don't think we need to see each other."

A couple of months later one of the guys at the station came up to me and said "I hear congratulations are in order for you." I said "Why?" He said "Aren't you and Jon getting married?" I almost threw up and said "Excuse me, no and I never want to hear his name or see his face again in my life." He said "I'm so sorry sweetie. I assumed it was you because you guys dated so long." I said "No, it's one of his slut's, Excuse me, Please, I've had enough of this in my face." He said "I'm so sorry". All the guys assumed it was you because we knew you were dating him for so long." I said "No. I don't know who it is. I really don't want to talk about him or this any more if you don't mind."

Jon called and asked "If he could come over to talk to me? I said "I think the talk is all ready all over town and there really is not anything else to say. You are marrying someone else and that's who has been in your house when you called me and asked me out previously what else do you think you need to say? I don't think there is anything else. Did I really cover the whole conversation in a nut shell for you? As far as I am concerned I think I did. There is nothing more or anything else to say." I then let him hear the Click of the phone.

While I was taking my paper work over to the courts today, some of the guys from the homicide unit decided to have a little fun and play like they were the Easter Bunny on me. When I got back from court I had this big basket on my desk saying "Peter Cottontail came by and decided to leave this for you for all your help that you have given us through out the year thus far. Thank you and stay sweet. Signed: From all the guys in Homicide." I went down stairs and told them they were quite welcome and that they did not need to buy me an Easter basket for helping them as that was my job." They said "we understand that but not when you keep getting spied on." I said "well I guess I can't take care of myself yet. Maybe she feels that my mom did not teach me how to, but if it does not stop soon, I will stop it just watch me."

The girls in my old unit gave me a little going away party even though it was only to another office, I was still in a different section. They gave me this beautiful crystal set at which I still have. We had a little lunch in the office instead of going out. They know that's what I would have liked more. I enjoyed being with them in our surroundings and being us. Where we could laugh and cut the jokes without insulting anyone else. That was really nice.

In my new section I had to give my new supervisor the information on my mother in regards to her illness. Remember as She was in the hospital across the street from the building from us so I went to see her on my dinner hour. There was this other person whom thought that I was saying something about her. She knew that I did a lot of crocheting and she asked me to do some for her for a wedding gift. I made a gift for her and then she gave me a big hassle about it. She said "I charged her too much money for the gift after we already agreed upon a price."

Now Trudy all of a sudden starts, with this nonsense that I'm saying that I'm her supervisor and I'm saying that she is taking home supplies and illegally using the computer in order to check up on her son, when I didn't even know that she had a son. I was accused of typing a letter to the director and placing it on his desk. The only letter I placed on the director's desk was the one about Kris referencing what she was going on with her and me and to try to get her to stop her nonsense of following me everywhere I went. What was Trudy talking about? Well all of a sudden I'm being called into Internal Review and being questioned about this letter about Trudy and I advised them that the only letter I gave my supervisor was about the entombment of my mother.

Now as it is in September and my mother's doctor advised us that she was not in remission. And I worked in a Section of the Department at the time we will call Systems. In December, she turned for the worst. I advised my current supervisor that my mother was extremely ill and was not expected to make it past Christmas.

She advised me that I had to put it in writing, what she was ill from and where her entombment would be. Now as I went through a surgical procedure myself in December as my mother was dying from cancer the doctors did not know if I had cancer at that time either.

My girlfriend Sue whom I have known since I was in sixth grade, she is my best friend and I called her up and we were talking about the situation. She said "I can not believe what you are going through sweetie. I would not put up with this much more. Is there not some kind of way that you can go higher to get her off your back?" I told her what I did but that it really did not work too well. We used to go driving down the street and sing to the radio till our hearts content. We had such fun. I remember when her first boyfriend gave her such grief and she wanted to move out of his house. She was so afraid that he would come home in the middle of the night or call here so she called me up and I went over with her and packed her up and told her to just keep moving and get it done and over with. We did this so quickly and she never forgot it.

I received a call from Jon's wife today. She said "It was an emergency. She called the office and gave her name and number and asked if they would call me and give me the name and number. She said it was an emergency. I just got done working another 12 hour shift. I do those a lot." My office called me and said Lee-Ann "I'm sorry and I know you probably just got home from traffic, or are just about to go to bed but I have an emergency phone call for you." I said "Okay, let me get some paper and pencil" "Go ahead I'm ready."

They gave me the number, then the name. There was quite a relief in my voice and my supervisor said "Oh sweetie I'm sorry that's not an emergency is it?" I said "No, not really. But thank-you and I will call and find out what this is all about." I hesitated to call as I was tired from working so many hours and I really wanted to sleep.

But I thought she wouldn't stop calling so I made the call and I asked for Mrs. Smith. She said "Speaking" I said "This is Lee-Ann, How can I help you? I don't have anything to say to you and there is really no emergency that you have that I need to hear from you, so if you don't want me to call your husband and have this stopped, you better stop now and never call me again." She said "I need to meet with you, my marriage depends on whether I can meet with you or not." I said "I don't think so. I haven't spoken to Jon since you two have been together." She said "I found these pictures of naked women on his bed and I need to know if any of them were you.

He really loved you before we got married." I said "That's funny, because if he really loved me then we would have been married. And for the record he never took pictures of me naked with candles all around me on his bed. That's just sick." Maybe that's what he was doing with the one in the red car. Who knows what was going on in those hours at the house while they were there.

I called my long time ago ex-boy friend to tell him that mom was sick and passed away. His name was Hery and he worked for Publix. When I called to tell him that she passed away, because she thought the world of him and him of her, he said "That is really weird because I knew something was wrong that day, I was so upset for some reason and I couldn't place why. Let me know when the services are and I will come." I said "I just thought you should know, but I don't know if it is really appropriate if you go to the services. But I appreciate it. My boyfriend will be there and it really will not be right.

I will let you know where she will be buried if you want to pay your respects later that will be okay." He understood and said "That this would probably be better that way because of the circumstances." I did not think that Hery should go to the funeral as he could never really get over me. He came back to me several times and wanted to marry me and I just could not do that. I loved him but I was not in love with him.

I also called Jon and told him because he knew her and respected her. He asked if he could come to the funeral. I said he could if he wanted to because I'm sure it would be around the department. However, if his wife asked how he found out, he could say "That he read it through one of the county bulletins. The one the director puts out and he called to say his Sympathy's because I didn't want her calling me again."

He said "What did you mean her calling you again?" I said "She called me a couple of times and wanted me to meet with her and I told her No. Then I said "Like when you told her you ran into me at the elevator at work. Little things like that Nothing big. I didn't dare tell him about the pictures. I actually hated him for this. I was going through enough. He wanted me to tell him what else she called me for. I could not tell him."

Three days before Christmas in 1986 my mother lay down from Cancer and never was able to get back up again. God rest her soul. I was there the weekend of her death. I spent the weekend at her home and came to work on Monday. I worked two jobs. I had a very Eire feeling that day. I called my mom and dads home every hour on the hour. My sister thought I was nuts. I went from my first job to the department and when I got there I called home and asked my sister again "Is Mom okay?" She said "I'll call if something happens, I said no, I have this awful feeling, and I can't explain it, Dear just bear with me. I love you okay."

When I got to the police department Tara came up to me and asked me if I was okay? She told me that I didn't look good. She asked me "if I had a bad weekend, what happened, your upset about something?" I told her what happened over the weekend. I just have this awful feeling something is going to happen. My girlfriend came up to me and said "are you Okay Lee-Ann you look really tired, what happened?" I told her that my mom took extremely ill, and that she was bed ridden and that her nurse said it was probably her last weekend before Christmas. Her nurse said "That she would not make it to see Christmas. Christmas was on a Wednesday and we were on Monday of the week. This was not easy to take as things were getting progressively worse.

I started crying and all of a sudden this stupid girl came up to us and said "Your not in very good control of your emotions and I told her if you do not want to go through that glass door head first I would suggest you move out of my face and leave me alone because you will not be able to get out of it alive. You do not get along with me and have no business in my face at this time in my life. I was so upset I felt like I could have put anyone in my face through a door without opening it.

When I was with my mother I was sitting and doing some needle point. She could not see at the last stage of her life but she could hear. I asked her "if she would like some Jell-o? " My sisters used to tease me when I was a little girl that it was a live and shake it on a spoon and I would scream until they took it away, so I asked her if she remembered that and if she did to squeeze my hand once. She did and if she wanted some of that red Jell-o to squeeze my hand once and I would get her some of that. She did this and I got her some. I would tell her what I was working on and it seemed to ease her as she would fall asleep and just relax. Her nurses would come by and check on her vitals and people from the church would stop over to say Hello.

I would describe the blanket that I was working on to her so she would be able to see the scenery in her mind. It was a little lady pushing a baby up the side walk to the house through some trees. It had birds and a sun on it. There were flowers on it and pretty blue clouds as well. This would make her smile. Today is Monday and I am at work and it is about six pm and my boss is sending me home because I need to be with my mom. I have this awful feeling something is going to happen and I just can not explain it. My boss is going to let Tara drive me home because she is the closest to me and because of the condition that I am in they are afraid that I would get into an accident, so they feel that it is better that I be driven down to my mother's home.

My sisters came over all weekend and we took turns taking care of her. We took shifts so that each of us had time to spend with her and share time and tell her things we wanted to say to her. She could not speak but she could hear us and it was so important that we could let her know that we loved her and that was our way of communicating to her was if she understood us was to squeeze our hand once for yes and twice for no. She was okay with that .

Christmas was on Wednesday. My sister was in a car accident and was in the hospital. I was trying to deal with all of this and work two jobs as well, I did not need the extra of the nonsense from these women.

I am at the hospital and I have to go in to see my sister as I told the doctor of our moms situation then I said "I haven't told her yet. I'm going in there now to tell her and I want to be alone to tell her the truth. I will not pull any punches with my sister about my mom. I didn't lie about the situation." Everybody was there on Sunday to see her and she got to hear all of her kids. I know this meant a lot to her. She needed to hear this as it was a comfort for her.

I am at home with my sister and we are sitting talking about her husband, son and daughter, when we hear my mom sigh. This is about eight o'clock at night. It was a strange night. It is about nine at night and I told her sis "you need to call who ever you need to call because mom is gone." She said "How do you know that?" I said "I haven't heard her sigh in an hour. I will go check her. But you need to call whom ever you need to call. My dad called the hospices and they came and took her out of the home.

I don't remember calling the station but they said "I called the station and advised them." About 3:00 am I showed up at the station to advise them of the passing and the final funeral arrangements they said I called but I don't remember calling however because I was so upset I just sat and talked with the girls I got along with and my supervisor.

When it came time to give the information for her services I told my supervisor that I would appreciate it if any of the girls that gave me grief in the office not to come to the funeral, as I would escort them out of the funeral home myself. I would not have the funeral director do this, it would be my pleasure, because if they could not respect me than they did not need to come and see the body that gave me life.

I felt that after all the problems that they caused I didn't want them there. Bob was living in South Carolina and it was not on my mind to call him and tell him the status of my mom so when he called me I did not know who he was on the phone when he started to talk. I had my second mom answer the phone and she asked who it was and then told him that I lost my mom and he said "he would come over" and I said "I would prefer not to have anyone over that particular night." She was there and that was who I really wanted to be with. He said " he would be over the next night" and I said " that would be fine as I did not know who I was talking to."

I did no t know if I was coming or going and I could not close my eyes so my second mom stayed with me as she lived above me and my second mom and dad understood very well what I was going though, he taught it was better that she stayed with me because I could not go to sleep as every time I tried to close my eyes I screamed at the thought of what I saw. The reality of my mom really being dead was too much for me the first night.

My old friend was there that I grew up with and I stayed with him as he could not go to the funeral home. He said "he wanted to remember her as she was when we were kids." I perfectly understood this. Bob came over the next day.

Tara and I would do a lot of things together. We would go shopping together and go on vacations together. We would spend the weekends at each others houses and help each other out. Her kids would come over to my house and sometimes I would make dinner for them. They would pick up movies and we would watch movies together. We always had fun . Tara came over and spent the night and my second mom went up stairs so when I tried to get some sleep someone was with me at all times.

In a meeting in the commanders office with the supervisors, Trudy, and myself, my supervisor (whose name was Diane) said, " It would have been better for all parties involved if you, Trudy, would have done your homework to find out what Lee-Ann really did type in her letter to me, because it really was only information about her mothers entombment." At this point, the director asked me "where I wanted to go in the department". I could transfer there without a two weeks notice, it was up to me.

My supervisor asked where they could send flowers and we asked that in lieu of flowers please send donations to the cancer society in memory of her for research for a cure for breast cancer. The department friends spread the word around the jail and the court house and there was as wonderful donation made in her memory for this. Thank you for the Donation.

Now do you remember the call from the ex-boy friend's wife, She called back the next day asking to speak to me again. She said "She needed to talk to me because Jon told her that he ran into me." I said "Look, he ran into me in the elevator and the doors could not close fast enough as far as I was concerned. I am totally upset abut what happened. Can't you leave things alone?" She still insisted on meeting me. Some people are so insecure about their marriage that I guess running into the ex-girlfriends isn't allowed, that you can't be friends. I don't understand that part. What I don't understand is that if you love someone how you can have someone else in the back door and then two moths later your married to them.

She said "Her marriage depended on whether I was one of these girls that were in the photos." I said "I feel sorry for you if that's what you base your marriage on then why did you marry him in the first place?" "You should be more stable with him than a bunch of photos and bring it up to him if you need to know who they are that bad. Leave me alone. There will be no more discussion on this matter. Do not call me or bother me any more or you will not like the other side of me. Do you understand? I really have more pressing things on my mind."

I have to go to an Arthritis doctor because my knees and hands are bothering me so bad that I cannot stand the pain any longer. They sent me to this one that is so good and nice that I really like him. His name is DR Minos. He says that I have severe Arthritis in my hands and knees and that I would have to start taking a lot of different kinds of medicine to get them to stop hurting so bad and swelling. This never affected my job as I would not let it. They had to drain my knees with a long needle and let me tell you that did not tickle. This was done twice and I swore that I would not let them ever do that again.

Tara and I took a road trip to Missouri, Tennessee, Alabama, Georgia, and Florida; we visited her family and mine. We saw Ruby Falls and Elvis Presley Estate in Tennessee. That is really something nice to see if you ever get a chance to see it. If you ever get a chance to climb the falls you should to that, it is truly beautiful for when you reach the center it is unbelievable. To think how Mother Nature creates some of these beauties and they have been there for centuries it is truly amazing.

When I would take my paper work over to the courts in the morning I was told of a position in the DUI Tape room and they always said "If I ever needed a new home to go to I was always welcome there." When the trouble started here, and the director told me that I could go wherever I wanted to, I transferred to the DUI Tape room. It was a small office and I thought it would be good for me at the time because of the loss of my mother and all the stress in my life. I needed to reduce some of that stress as my blood pressure was starting to get out of control.

I took classes at the library to teach illiterate people how to read. I received a certificate from them. I did this on my own time after work. When the department found out, they requested a copy of the certificate and it went into my file. I received a commendation at the department.

I had a student from the library and she wanted me to go to her home land with her to see where she was born and where she grew up. I thought that was pretty interesting, so I made my next vacation plans around that and we took two weeks and went. We went to Jamaica for two weeks. It was nice.

This was a volunteer position. I did not need outside employment approval for this. We went to Duns River Falls and climbed the water fall then went swimming in the river. We had dinner at the local taverns and danced at the nightclubs. We shopped at the side shops on the side walks. Most of the shops close up at six o'clock in the evening, so if you don't have a fancy hotel room to stay in or are not staying in a resort or with some friends on the island, there really is not much to do.

We were with some very wealthy people so at least we had something to do. We were out sight seeing and we were on this mountain side when all of a sudden this guy comes out with a shot gun and tells us to get off his property or else he would push us off the side of the mountain in the car.

I thought this guy was just trying to scare us off, and the next thing I knew he was actually pushing the car. I told my friend "lets get out of here and go someplace else or we will be dead. I did not come here to go through this. If this is what this trip is going to be like, then take me back to the airport and I will go back home now." "You can catch a different flight home and I will talk to you later." I was so mad that I did not want to speak to her because they thought it was a joke.

I said "whether you think this is a joke or not the man wants us off his property and that is quite clear. We do not have the right to be here and I do not know where I am or how to get out of here, so take me back to where I am suppose to be or to the airport and I will go home. This was no joke." And this is not what I came for, if you have any thing in your plans to hurt me this will be your biggest mistake….

That really ruined the whole trip and the friendship between us and her daughter. I still taught in the library. I told the library that she could read when she wanted to, she just chose not to, she just wanted to say that she changed the words around when she wanted to. If you can tell me the same sentence six times in a row and then three times later and not realize that you did when I was quizzing you on them, then you just wanted attention and I was not there to give her attention I was there to teach.

While we were doing this at the library I had another mother ask "if I would charge her to teach her daughter to do her homework?" I asked her "what the problem was?" She said "she did not know" I said "bring her to the library and let me sit with her so that I can find out what the problem was. If it was homework related or if it is that there is no one at home to be there if she needed help with her homework. Sometimes it's just the attention and if that is the case you are more than welcome to bring her to the library to us on our library days, so she feels that she is getting added attention for her homework and this might pick up her grades in school."

I don't mind and you can see if it helps. She said "I will try it. I have to do something as I am a single parent and she is left at home alone and I know she doesn't really like it that much." When the next report card came her grades were all B's. Her mother was overwhelmed. She could not thank me enough for the time spent with her daughter. I told her it was no problem. She said "it was your time, and you volunteer it. That is what makes it so special." I told her I love kids and that is why I did it." We made a little celebration dinner for both ladies and they were very happy that day.

Cheryl, Jose, Mom and Dad Pen, and Marie are helping me move into my first house. This is really exciting. I'm having my first little dinner party in the house. The girls from work that I got along with were coming over. How exciting.!!! I haven't seen them for a while. This will be nice. I have asked Sgt. Kenct and his wife to come however with the nonsense that is going on he said "He wasn't sure that would have been a good idea but greatly appreciated the invitation." No matter how hard they try to break up a persons friendship some people just didn't let that happen. Once you earn someone's respect, it's pretty hard to break it down.

Sue was at my first house and she was helping me move into the house. She was moving the kitchen boxes around and asking me where this box was supposes to go and where should this box go. Then she would say sweetie where does this box go and should I put this one here? I told her "to do what she thought best" and she would say "not in your kitchen." We then laughed for hours over that joke as she would say you are too picky about where things should be. I said "if I did not like it I would change it later. I was getting the help now and I appreciate it so why would I knock a gift horse in the mouth?" Then we would go get some lunch and come back and finish the rest this would give us a little break.

I am at the house and my girlfriend came over and I was working on fixing it up. I was taking the kitchen apart and changing the decor. I had to redecorate the whole house as I bought an estate home and I had a lot of fun doing this little by little. I worked the diner so I could do the redecorating and it would not cost too much money. My friend Lou needed a place to rent with her kids so she stayed in the spare rooms that I had. Since I had extra rooms so why not?

The house was plenty big enough for all of us and we got along great. I was in the kitchen when my girlfriend came in and saw me up on the ladder taking the ceiling down so it was smooth and getting it ready for painting. Then I was going to take off the cabinets and get them ready to be repainted and change the knobs. The next thing was the walls needed painting as do all walls no matter where you go. Then I had to hang doors in the bedrooms. I had hard wood floors in the bedrooms and the living room. In the front room and the dinning room was old tile that had to be picked up.

I had to hammer this up with a small hammer. I think I will have ceiling fans with lights installed now. Boy is this starting to shape up mighty nice. Now the kitchen floor and a small counter top specially made by my brother in law will be installed. This really looks nice. Well I will have to put carpet down in the living room as I cannot take the hardwood floors with the Arthritis I suffer from in my feet. I have a bookcase in the office and my nick -knacks on the shelves up top this really brings out the room a lot. I do the yard work myself. It takes a lot of the stress out of me. I am enjoying fixing up my little house as it is an accomplishment for me. I started saving every bit I could from when I lived in that two bedroom apt the size of a garage apt.

I lived like that for eight years so this was a big step for me. Loren came over today and I was working on the house. She could not believe that I knew how to do carpenter work. When she saw me sanding down the ceiling and hammering the floors she asked me where I learned how to do this work? I told her that my father taught me how to do it when I was a young kid. I would work side by side with him and that is how I learned to use these tools.

Lou told me that she wanted to move out with her boyfriend and that she felt that there was not enough room to have him live with both of us in the same house. I said "that was no problem." I understood. When Bob would come over he did not feel comfortable with this situation anyway, but I did not tell her that. Why should I, it was not his house it was mine."

# CHAPTER 5
# 1987

WHEN I TRANSFERRED INTO the DUI Tape room in the Court Liaison Section of the Department, in January of 1987 I took a transfer effective to this unit. My immediate supervisor was Sgt. Kend. He was an extremely nice person. Very helpful and if you needed anything he was the kind of person that would give you the shirt off his back. When I started in this room, the room had boxes, and boxes of tapes not lined up on shelves and not in any particular kind of order. We got the room in order and put the records cross referenced on the computer in order to look up names and case numbers to find the tapes faster.

My co worker Becky had a severe problem dealing with friendship among co-workers. She could not handle someone knowing more than her. As I was in the process of buying my first house and Sgt. Kend would say to me "Before you sign any paperwork that I was not sure of if I wanted him to look it over and let me know if there was something else I should do." Just out of friendship and not to get in trouble with something I might regret later.

Becky thought she was being left out so she starting causing a lot of problems. She called Mrs. Kend at home and told her that Sgt. Kend and I were having an affair. Becky did not like the fact that I would put information in the computer upstairs and would get upset. I was going on a vacation, so she wanted to enter the information into the computer saying this way it would not get backed up. What difference did it make if you are paid to file the tapes or enter the information in the computer? If your job is to file the tapes, and label them why must you put the information in the computer when you have not been trained to do so?

I would make air popped popcorn for lunch and Sgt. Kend occasionally used to have some. Some times the Judge would come off the bench and ask if he could have some and I would say "Sure, I would make him some as well." We had our own little fan club.

Well she wanted to input the information in the computer while I was on vacation, and in doing so she dropped 100 to 200 files. This was realized when I had to find a case number for a common name that should have had listed about seventy five to maybe one hundred times in the system, and it was no where to be found. When I brought this to the supervisor's attention, and tried to find them in the computer we could not believe it was done because of jealously.

This is just child's play and is not necessary. This took me approximately three weeks of overtime to re-enter all the files back into the computer. What ever place of employment you have you share the work load with your co-workers this should not be a threat that what ever your job was or your classification was you help where ever you could.

She told the Lt. that I was not letting her enter things into the system because I wanted to be the only one to enter the records into the system. When the Lt. saw what happened it was a horse of a different color so to say. He was not happy when she insisted on trying to enter information into the system. He told her that she could not do this part of the job any more and that her job consisted of the room down stairs and dealing with the officers and the tapes. The fact that the room was made much nicer. That the office down stairs was no longer just a bunch of boxes and boxes of tapes. That it was a nice office to work in and that the officers like to come to it because it makes it worth their while. She should not mind going to work there and should to stop causing so much trouble.

I still worked my part time job at the diner. I really enjoyed working there. It was more a sanity reliever than anything after the nonsense I was going through at the department. I am at work today at the dinner and it is a Wednesday. Boy we had lines out the door and around the corner of the restaurant for a fish and clam fry night all you can eat special. It was great. The customers were as usually very friendly and the tips were good too. This kind of work you really do not mind doing.

Now while I'm at the department again and we had a little radio and you talked to the officers when they came to the window or called up and requested a copy of a tape for court. When I got back from entering the records into the system, I always let her go out and walk around so that she wouldn't get board. I would tell her "Why don't you maybe go listen in so your not bored and I'll tell Sgt. that you are down the hall or in the bathroom."

It will be no problem to give you a break, but she didn't like that. She thought she was missing something. Especially if the Sgt. would be sitting and talking to me when she came back. It could be about a case he was sitting in on and or listening to how nice a day it was. Just anything to see how your day was going and she would be so upset. Sometimes I would tell the Sgt. that Maria took a break from the boredom and go sit in a court case for a while because she was cooped up in this room by herself and he didn't mind. He actually agreed with me because of the trouble she caused.

When she went to the tape room it would leave her there by herself. I'm sure nobody likes being by yourself, but you get paid to do things, I can't help that. What difference did it really make if your job is to file tapes, or label tapes, or copy tapes?

You are getting paid no matter what you are doing. When an officer needs a tape for court in a hurry then you need to get it or if they need copies for court we had to make them as well. Sometimes the officers would stop by just to say hello in between court cases to pass the time which was fine because the dread of the location could really get on your nerve.

It would make the boredom go by a little faster. We would have unit holiday parties and everybody would make a dish and pull names for a grab gift. That was nice and it was fun. We all wonder who would pull Becky's name because if I did, it would cause such a problem that I would have to change the name with someone else. If I pulled her name either one of the secretaries would change with me or the Sgt would always change so I did not have to buy her something that way it did not cause any additional troubles. That is such child play and I cannot stand to work like this but there is nothing I can do. This woman will not stop her nonsense.

I am at my sisters Dairy Queen and my ex-boy friend came into the back of the store and wanted to talk to me. He said "I have to talk to you abut something." I said "Jon, let me tell you something this has been eating at me for a long time. When your wife called me and said she wanted to meet me, do you remember that?" He said "yes." I said "Well it was because she wanted to know if I was among the ladies in the pictures of naked women that you took with candles around your bed. I told her that you never took naked pictures of me and that she did not have to make sure that I was not one of them and your marriage to her was not solid enough evidently or she would not have to come running to me to find out if I was one of these ladies.

Also this made me sick to think that you were that type of person and that is what you were doing when you would not answer your door when you made a date with me and there were other peoples cars parked outside of your house several times. I hated you for what you put me through, and how you made me feel. I am seeing someone else and he would not stand for something like that. Please leave me alone.

The next day at work at the DUI tape room, I was approached by a city Officer and asked to find a tape that was missing and locate it for court by cross referencing the names and case numbers. In doing this the city Officer and supervisor gave me a commendation for finding this tape and making it available for court. And getting this done in a timely manner. Becky did not like this in the least. Sgt. Kend was tickled pink.

We receive unit commendations from the Judges and the Jail for having things done in a timely manner. Our unit would have our paperwork done in appropriate manners. We would have specials at the holidays. We would make parties and make plates, bring in covered dishes and have office parties. We would invite the Judges, the secretaries, and the people from the jail. It was a lot of fun.

It is a bright sunny day today and the Lauder Air Show was being held across the street from us. We watched the show from the beginning until the end. The ending of the show at sunset was spectacular. Watching the planes come in formation was something to see.

While we watched the show all we had to do is put chairs out side and watch it. They would come around the back of the house and go in the runway from the west side of the airport. The firs time I heard this come over the house I though the roof was coming off. We watched this for eight years. I loved my little apartment. We made Barbeques and little parties while we watched this shows.

My Lt., Carney called me into the office and in closed doors with no witnesses and accused me of saying "You are having an affair with Sgt. Kend and you will stop or else." You will stop calling him at home. You will stop meeting him. You are not allowed to talk to him about anything personal. You are not allowed to talk to him unless it is work related. This is my Sgt if I need him for any thing how am I supposed to get a hold of him? "You are not allowed to talk to him in the courtrooms.

You are not allowed to beep him to the DUI room. If I had a problem I had to call up stairs and tell someone else and have them tell Sgt. Kend so he could come and help fix the problem." Sgt. Kend came to the DUI tape room and Becky was out sick one day, he said "Have I done something to offend you?" I said "You are really being very silly, you're the kindest person I've met in this department why would you ask such a question?" He replied "because you haven't been very talkative lately."

I advised Sgt Kend of this accusation and he could not believe what he was hearing. He told me that our friendship meant a lot to him and he told his wife what was being said "she could not believe this lie either." He told me that I could talk to him any time I wanted to." Sgt. Kend took ill and could not join us at our Christmas party,

Lt. Carney asked "Me to bring all the office gifts to his house." How ironic I'm being accused of having an affair with him and then the same individual turns around and have me bring the office Christmas gifts to their house. Just a bunch of hypocrites and of course these accusations as usual would be made behind close doors with no witness.

I was advised to find another home where I would be transferred waving my two weeks notice. I was then pulled out of the DUI'S tape room and worked the phones in Court Liaison. I later learned that Sgt. Kend had passed away from cancer.

He never smoked or drank, but as they say the good always die young. God bless you Sgt. Kend. When you don't do anything to these people, why do you have to leave? Yet they think they have the upper hand on everyone. Well one day they will have to answer for all the wrong they have done, if not to me but to a higher power that truly sees and I believe that they will have to pay for it. What goes around comes around.

You know its really funny that these people always do this nonsense behind closed doors. In meetings with no witnesses so what they say when it's against them will of course have no witnesses. However this one had a witness and I am truly surprised that this person would put up with such bull shit. Maybe she did not want to stand up and accounted to higher authorities on it, but you have to truly wonder if she can rest at night in peace for all that they have done to others. Only I don't know about this sly move and just how much it goes or just how far yet!!!!!!!!!!!!

# CHAPTER 6

I'M ALREADY TOO FAR into this retirement fund to let it go, so maybe this division will be different. Let me try this with an open mind and see how it goes. My girlfriend used to tell me that she could not take any more of the non-sense that she was going through and I did not understand what she was talking about. I'm meeting my new bosses today and they seem to be nice people. There's a lady named Jill in the administration office, and she's really nice. And there's a secretary in the General Investigation Unit, her name is Shirley and she is nice. Most of the other people I'm meeting seem to be nice as well. Well that's what I thought about the other places that I worked at for the Department. That seems to be the general concept of this place. Show the two faces of eve. Be nice when you first arrive and then show your true colors later.

I started in the Doal Station in an Old Air Port Hanger. I believe it was in either 1988 or 1989. When I started in this station I had no training of what desk operations were. I thought this was going to be exciting. I had to teach myself how to work the desk, use the radio, and write reports, by trial and error. Upon teaching myself how to do this work, I had a few instances occur.

My co-worker who was to teach me the desk was always sleeping in the property room or in the bathroom because of an illness she had. It is eight o'clock in the morning and I am doing a background check on a lady when a hit for a missing person report came up in the system, from about twenty years prior to the date. She had walked away from a hospital and was reported missing. No-one ever called the police to report that she showed up at home, so she remained in the system for twenty years.

It just happens that I caught it that day. When I told my Sgt that I had a missing person recovery from twenty years ago he could not believe it. Once it was confirmed and released from the system he said "that was a good catch Lee-Ann, and how did you do that? What made you so sure that it was her? After all it was twenty years ago?" I said "Her name was the same, the date of birth was the same, I asked if she was ever at the location from where she was reported missing and if she ever knew that she had been reported as a missing person.

And if there were any scars, marks or any other identify marks that could make a positive identification of this being her. She said "She was at the hospital and took a cab home," so when someone reported her missing they never called the police to report that she had been recovered so she stayed in the system as a missing person until she came into the police station for a clearance letter for a job.

She would have never known that she was reported as a missing person if she did not need that letter, if she did not walk into the station that particular day. Timing is of the essence. There was never anything said about it or anything done as to putting anything in my file about making a commendation on this however if I were an officer they would have made an commendation about making such a find that a twenty year old case was solved. All you get is good catch when you are a civilian.

These kinds of things are not necessarily told to the media and alerted so that the public can be educated that when you call the police on a missing person and they come home you have to call them so they can be reported as recovered. This is an important event so that they do not sit in the system for years like this poor lady. That is also how all those missing and unidentified body parts are placed as well and stay for years.

I would teach Officers how to finger print people and help in printing people. I never took a class to teach officers or civilians how to finger print people, I just watched finger print technicians do there jobs and that is how I learned. I asked questioned and watched and some would teach. Not too much ink or the prints are not readable. Not too little ink or you cannot see the lines or the deltas or the swirls. That is how I learned to take prints. I would assist in sting operations doing paper work and running checks on people.

I would do inventories of property, and check to see how many reports I could start writing. When I came in the first thing I was suppose to do was to check the screen and see how many reports were needed to be written and to clear up the units on the road so that the new crew could be in roll call and see what was expected of them or if any new training was to be done and who had to be going where.

Some times I would write maybe six or seven reports first thing in the morning within the first hour and then do the inventories. I am there to work not for a beauty contest or a popularity contest, so it doesn't bother me any if someone does more or less than me. If I am teaching myself how to write these reports and learn the radio and do the desk operations then I don't see why other people cannot do the same.

When I first came on the desk I had to pick up a report and look at it, take it to the screen and fill in the blanks. Then take it to the officer on the desk and ask what I was missing so that I would learn. This was the only way to learn how to write the reports and the fastest way, and when I had to teach the other person on the desk she did not believe me. I understand when you don't want to there is a difference. When you want to act like you are helpless and that everyone around you has to do everything for you or keep telling you the same thing over and over again, then why are you there?

I took a hand held radio home with the permission of my Sergeant to learn the codes of the radio and to get used to the language so that I could understand what was being said and to be able to write reports and to be able to answer the dispatcher back. I wanted to be able to answer her without having to keep asking the officer on the desk what to tell her every time she would ask us to do something and that was a good way to learn.

I'm at the diner and there is this customer that is very belligerent. He is getting very loud with other customers. Yelling at them for no reason and screaming at them. Telling them that they don't have the right to look at him and really getting out of hand. One of the cooks came off the line to see if he could get him under control. I went over to the Phone and called 911 and left the phone line open. This customer jumped the cashiers line and started for the cooks line where the knifes were. By then the Police were there. The customer's family was with him, and they could not get him under control. When the Police finally got him outside and in handcuffs he stopped struggling and then all of a sudden stopped breathing.

They called for fire rescue but it was too late, the customer died. They had to do an investigation and rope off the parking lot. They came in and questioned everyone. We told them what we knew. That he came in and "started to order his dinner and was talking to his family and then he just started getting loud and out of control for no reason. That's when we called and left the line open so that we could get someone here and he would not know that we called the police. He told us not to call the police when he started for the cook's line but he didn't know that I already had done so."

They came back and told us about a month later that the customer was on cocaine and that is why he passed away. There was nothing we could have done for this gentleman. That was pretty scary and they offered us there physiological services if anyone needed it. I guess that was okay, I don't know if the family took them up on it, I know I did not because I worked for the department and I did not want anyone to know what was going on.

When I get off work it will be 7:00 am and then I will go home and get about six hours sleep. My friend would call me every day at 12:00 and tell me that "This was my wake up call to make sure that I was awake." One day in particular I got up and went to get into the shower. When I did, I lost my balance and I fell on the slide of the shower doors. Then I fell into the shower. I had such black and blues by the time I got to the station and I was not really coherent about what was going on around me.

One of the Sgt's. came up to me and asked me what happened to me or who beat me up? I said "No one beat me up, I fell in the shower and I tried to break the fall, but I couldn't and I fell anyway making it worst as you can tell." I said "Please don't touch me, it really hurts like heck." Sgt. Springfield didn't like this too well. I really wasn't concerned as I was working my part time job that was approved and everything was in order. I was a little dizzy because of the fall so I really did not want to get back in the car and go get lunch. It just happened that the Sgt's were going out to lunch and they asked me if they could bring me something back so I would have something to eat.

They all knew that I was hurt and that I was feeling a little dizzy from the fall, and also that my Sgt was giving me such a hard time so they just offered to bring in lunch to me. That was very nice of them. They brought me back a salad and then when I went to pay for it none of them would let me give them the money. They asked me again "Are you sure that no one beat you up?" I said "Yes, I really fell in the shower as I only got four hours sleep". "There was an incident on my other job and if you need to verify it check with Sunlakes Lakes, we had a deceased person in the parking lot and I was able to leave because I work here and some of the guys know me."

They said "are you working tomorrow?' I said "Yes and I need to get some sleep or I will not make it so could you interview me now and get it over with so I could go and then go to work." Everything was okay because I was the one that called the police when the gentleman lost his cool and the next thing we knew he was fighting in the restaurant.

With the customer was out of control all I did was to go back to my tables to try and keep my customer's as calm as possible. That's why I got such little sleep. Wouldn't you know it that my Sgt would not believe it that it was true and she called Haven Lakes district to see if they had such a situation occur in the district, on the midnight shift and when she found out that it was true, the other Sgt's said "Now leave her alone, if you say something to her or cause her any grief over this we will say and cause you grief. You now know that this is the truth and you cannot pick on her for it so just leave her alone."

As I'm working the desk one day, and this lady comes in asking for an Officer, we will call him Jones, I can't remember his last name, and I said "I believe he has gone for the day." He worked midnights. I had no Idea who he was. She replied "I know he's here, I can see him from the tower. She started walking in the back of the station and as I really didn't know who she was, I said "Madam I'm sorry, but I believe he has gone for the day.

I will try to page him again but you cannot just Strom in the station." She replied very hostile, "Well, you don't know who I am and you can loose your job by not letting me back there." I replied "Why, are you God?" I contacted my Sgt. and advised him of the situation and he stated "It was okay, because she was only his girlfriend and she was not allowed to just enter the station at any time like she thinks she can."

I am in the process o f buying my second house now, so I am staying at my girlfriend's house for a couple of months. Her kids loved this. We were very close. They of course did not want to put their toys away at night before going to bed, so I got a big garbage bag and told them "Any toys I picked up I would be placed in the bag and I would put this bag in the trash if not picked up in the morning. I did this in front of them so that they would learn to put their toys away." The next two nights they were putting their toys away by the end of the T.V. programs that came on and they had their teeth brushed. Their mom could not believe what I had done. She asked me "How did you do this?" So I told her. I told her anything is possible if you want it done. I would watch the kids at night and she would be with them in the day. I would feed them dinner and bathe them.

I would help them with their home work. I would read them a story. I would rock the baby to sleep. She had a Christening for the baby and there were too many people at the party. Everybody wanted to hold the baby but she was too upset. All of a sudden she started crying and she would not stop.

My girlfriend went to pick her up and try to console her but she could not calm her down. She asked her mom to try and she could not calm her down, then she asked the dad to try and daddy couldn't do it either. Then she said "Lee-Ann", could you pick up Irene she is having a bit of trouble with all these people and she just does not know what is going on." I said "sure, not a problem.

I then picked her up and said to the baby what's the matter sweetie its okay I have you. It's me baby." She looked at me and held on for dear life and would not go to anyone else. I said to her "its okay, I have you baby. Don't worry." She was calm the rest of the afternoon. The other two kids were great. They would help me with anything I asked after I showed them that once we put our toys away after a certain hour we could watch a little T.V. and then go to sleep.

They used to like to talk and talk and talk in the bedrooms and I would tell them to "cut the tea parties out" and they would laugh and I would tell them that's enough and to go to sleep. About ten or fifth-teen minutes later they would be sleeping.

While I am working at the Doal Station when we are in an emergency mode operation. When working this emergency mode operation on the desk with officer Night who sitting across from me and we were talking when all of a sudden, he reached over and put his hand down my shirt while. I became so enraged that I walked off the desk STORMED into the Sgt. office and spoke to Sgt Haknn telling him of the situation advising him that the next time Officer Night touches me, I won't be responsible of the outcome I might just fly of and hit him, however he will not like the consequences. Sgt Haknn" asked me to tell him to come back to the Sgt office." I said "I will not say anything to him, I have nothing to say to him except to drop dead." Sgt. "If you have something to say to him you need to call him backs here yourself. He then told me to take the long way around the station to get back to the front of the station so he could have time to have him answer the phones.

This way he would have to answer the phone and it would be the call for him to report the Sgt office. There was nobody else around when he did this so there was no witnesses to see what he did. When I got back to the desk he went back to the Sgt office and I did not say a word to him. My face was as red as it could possibly be, as I did not know at the time that I was suffering from high blood pressure. I am the type that will keep everything in and not let it out.

However, I will not stand for anyone touching me where they do not belong. I told the Sgt that I am not any ones touch me doll and that I am not here for anyone to put their hands on in any manner. I am not a sex toy to any one and this better stop.

There was this other Sgt. whose name was Sgt. Fieldgreen. He had an officer on his squad who was having personal problems and he was telling me to have his wife go to the Internal Review Section, to handle what she was trying to bring into the station. I did not know what she wanted to talk about, as it was not my business, and I really didn't feel it was anyone else's business. I really think Sgt. Fieldgreen was correct in sending her to this section. If I would have known that I could have gone there for what they put me through I would have went there myself, however, since I didn't know WELL they now can read just how ignorant they really are.

Sgt. Fieldgreen has since left the department and from what I heard has a florist shop in PA. I used to work under his supervision. He is extremely nice, and very easy to work for. He said to me "If I ever needed a job, he would have no problem letting me work for him and putting me in a management position in his shop because he knows his shop would run like a well oiled machine." I might just get the notion to surprise him and come there one day.

Sometimes someone would ask for a phone number and if for some reason unconsciously I would say it out loud or if someone was looking for something and couldn't find it and I was able to find it I was accused of under minding the Sgt's because a higher rank asked a question which I would know the answer to. I wouldn't say that is necessarily undermining someone.

That is just not being able to say that maybe someone can find something a little faster than you can. Or maybe just unconsciously it comes out. When the officers at the desk would need a phone number for something, they would come to me first, and if I didn't know it I knew where to find it or would have it on the phone because of dialing it so many times. Is that under minding or being efficient????????

I was advised by Lt. Socar to go to the Lt.'s office at which time Lt. Socar stated in a meeting "That I made him sick and that he was to the point that he could throw something at me to cool off his anger. Lt. Socar then threw a stapler from across the room after making this statement at me. At which time I asked if he was finished. I got up and walked out of his office and went home as it was the end of my shift.

They transferred my co-worker to another section that was less demanding and less stressful so she would be able to get her health back. That left the position opens for another PRS. Because I was senior to her, I had to teach her how to do the job. There was never any extra pay involved for any teaching although FTO's get a pay increase to train. After this individual, Heather, was hired everything changed. If you think things don't change because your heavy, boy your so very wrong!!!!!!!!!

She of course did not know how to write a report, answer the radio, fingerprint someone,or do a background check. I know I was the senior PRS, so this was their way of saying "That it was my job to teach her." That was not the problem, but when it is held against you because you are heavy, and your co-worker is skinny, that's all she wrote. Well when I had to go to the secretaries office to answer phones so they could go to lunch, because I got bored, I would bring a police radio, listen and take down information to write reports if I could.

Well this got to Heather, and she did not like it, so she would complain that I was taking more reports than her. I came in to work an hour before her shift and I would check the screen to see what calls were holding, I would write what reports I could in that hour because that is what we were suppose to do. If someone came in from off the streets I would attend to them, she did not like this either.

If I fingerprinted more people than her, I was wrong. For what, for just doing my job. I am not lazy like others who thinks working for the government is a free load job. They would do what they needed to get by and get good pay for it, since there was no quota to meet. Instead they would talk and play and hang out so as not to get anything done. However, my parents always taught me to work for my pay. That being lazy never got you anywhere, so with this training I did my job and others too because if I didn't it was backlogged.

# CHAPTER 7

I BROUGHT THIS SITUATION to my supervisors attention, and he told her "Heather, if she gets bored sitting in the secretaries office and takes reports off the road units hands, and she which are able to be written by the phone to free a unit for a more pressing calls, there is nothing wrong with that. She is not doing anything wrong." When you are sitting in for the secretaries office you should take a radio so that you could learn the language better and write reports, that way you would pick up the language faster. When Lee-Ann first got here that is what she did and that is how she learned the language. She took a radio home and listened to it so that she could learn the language faster and understand the calls. Maybe you should take one home and listen to it so you can pick up the language faster as well.

She did not like this and believe me because I was over weight, which had a lot of bearing on things when it should not have, I was advised that I would be placed on the afternoon shift. You think that weight does not have a lot of bearing on things in the public sector but it truly does.

These people can make your life miserable. Such saying things like "does a pig eat too much or if they didn't chew your food so fast it might get a chance to digest, or does it just sits there. Comments like if we stick the balloon with a pin will it deflate and so when can we do it?!!!!!!!!!!!!!". Or when you walk does your skin rub and turn you on, or does your mate like it when you make love to roll with the meat for you eat enough for the two of you!!!!!!!!!!!!!

I had a family of five people come in to be finger printed one day. I suppose to split (?) the family in half just to make Heather happy so she would be okay with me helping five people. I don't think so even if I could which I humanly cannot what is the problem. So I finger printed the entire family. She got so mad, and then came to me and said ""Why didn't you let me help you?" I said "I'm sorry, what do you mean, with the family, I'm confused. Where did I need help?" I had already written six reports earlier that morning and that's what had gotten her mad. That morning however, I was to work an hour earlier than her.

It was just a busy morning, nothing anybody could have done or predicted. Since my shift was for me to be in one hour before hers and to leave one hour before her, and lunch hour so that she would get the chance to have written six or eight or even ten reports more than I, I would not have gotten upset with it. But she could not handle anyone doing more work than her only because it made her look bad. Then get off your lazy but and try to learn the job and do it right.

It showed just how lazy she really was and she did not like that. She would go to the Sgt and cry that I would take all the reports and not let her have any. Look at the times that they came in and the times that they were there and see if the dispatcher did not ask if the desk officer or personal could not handle any of the calls holding at the time to see if they could be cleared up.

Was I suppose to say, Oh I have to wait for Heather because she will get upset that she could not write some of these reports, so I need to leave some of them for her? I don't think that either the dispatcher or the Lt would be to happy to have me tell them that the reason I did not answer the Lt or the dispatcher because Heather did not have her quota for the day, so I just wrote the reports. I can not help whose feelings got hurt because I did my job. No matter where I worked I have always done my job and helped others with what ever I could.

I was asked by the Captain of the station (Bourgain) if I wanted to go to afternoons. I was not interested in that as I had a part time job and wanted to stay on days, but in no uncertain words I was told I would go to afternoon shift whether I wanted to or not. Only because

Heather was much skinnier than I she stayed on days and I wound up on afternoons.

Trust me that was one of the reasons, the other was that the captain really cared for her instead of me. I never did anything to him. I just did not get along with his house maid, my Sgt and that was the only reason. I tried to say that I had seniority and that did not go anywhere. That's the way it's supposed to be.

I tried to say that because of my second job I needed the hours so could I stay on days in order to work my two jobs. They gave me the ultimatum which was which one was more important. They wanted financial records and why I needed to work two jobs. Get real. Having a house and trying to keep up everyday life by yourself on one job is just not that easy. They did not do this to any one else but me. They would have worked around anyone else's schedule but mine.

When the Doal station moved from an old annex building to the new headquarters building. I assisted in setting up the front desk, files, and vehicles information. On several occasions I asked to go back on days but as usually to no prevail. While working for the Doal Station I worked for a Sgt Springfield. She did not like nor get a long with me at any point in time. I was on a diet for health reasons and when I lost a lot of weight boy how the attitudes changed.

I lost a total of 90 lbs. One of the girls said to me "I have a dress I think you should try since you lost all your weight." She brought it into the station and I tried it on. When I came out of the bathroom, a lot of heads turned including Lt. Oto's saying "My goodness is that Lee-Ann." Well it had a slit up the side of the dress almost to the hip and that's not me, I don't care how much weight I loose. I went back into the bathroom and took the dress off. Now if the dress made that much difference, my personality didn't change at all. My girlfriends gave me a gift for glamour shots for my birthday that year and took me out to lunch.

I had some of the pictures made up. One of the girls in the office asked me for a picture and placed it on her desk in the General Investigations Unit. One of the detectives came up to her and said "Shirley, who is that?" She said "You know who that is." He said "No I don't." She said "Yes you do." He said Shirley I really don't know who that is, who is she?" Shirley said "It's Lee-Ann." He said "No way, that's not her she doesn't look like that". Shirley said "She does when she dresses up and when she is going out, you just don't know her."

I have been with the same person whom is not a cop, for a long time. He would call on the other county line and when my Sgt would answer it, she was so rude to him. Sgt. Springfield did not like me and caused a lot of problems. She wrote me up because she would not listen to any answers I had when I was asked questions. When she realized I was connected to an officer on the department, my troubles got worse. She did not like the fact that I was the sister in law to an officer in the department.

At this point in my life, my arthritis doctor has advising me that I am going to have to start using a handicap parking permit and to be parking closer to buildings. I am having too many difficulties walking malls. My arthritis is starting to get worse in my knees and it is very painful and can put you down in a heart beat and that is no fun. I only use the sticker when I have to so, I can get the exercise the rest of the time.

Even at the department because I don't want the hassles. I asked him not to let them know so they will not try to let me go out on a disability yet. I have had to take all different kinds of medications for my arthritis. I have taken everything from ant-inflammatory to gold from the most common nsaids to prednisone. I am now on more advanced medicines for arthritis. I am taking methatrexate and Remicade. These are very hard medications to take and two other medicines for arthritis as well.

This is just so I can keep functioning on a daily basis. Like just to be able to hit the keys on a computer and be able to write this book. Or comb your own hair, or brush your teeth, maybe even do a button up on your shirt that is the hardest one for me. I cannot do a button on my shirt and this I hate. It is very painful to walk up a flight of stairs.

There are days when I am parked in the handicap parking spots in malls and some people will say to me "Are you aware that this is a handicap parking space? I would just look at them and say "Is it your business?" My back and legs hurt so bad I cannot walk the malls as I used to be able to do. I have a handicap tag issued by the state that I live in so it really is none of their business.

As I told you Sgt Sringfield was not happy at all that my brother in law was the president of the PBA. When he ran, she would say things, like well why don't you ask the horses mouth, if her brother-in-law is running for president? What's the status of his running? Where's the campaign headquarter' held at? I would not embrace the idiot with any answers. Any questions asked, I simply stated, "You need to call the P.B..A. hall, the number is 705-555-5555. They will answer all your questions.

At the time he ran there was a Hurricane that hit and it was named Andrew. I helped by putting flyers out in officers mail boxes for advertisements. I asked the Commander if I could and he told me it was okay. When he made the office, of course my Sgt. had her nasty mouth saying "Why don't you ask the Bitch if he made the President or not?" I just said "Call the P. B. A. hall and find out who the new P. B. A. President is if you can't be nice with your mouth. I didn't count the votes so I wouldn't know."

One day an officer called the station wanting to speak with the Lt. I transferred the call through to his car phone and after seventeen rings he did not pick up the line. I went back on the line and advised him that the Lt. did not pick up the call. Off. Xavier (SRT) wanted me to give him an (02) and per SOPS were not allowed to give 02's on the air.

The officer asked to speak to the officer on the desk (officer Quintan) and when I advised him that the phone was for him, instead of him picking up the phone he called the Lt. Wade's car phone, and the Lt(Wade). Picked up the phone at which time, I advised the officer to pick up the line again and the officer hung up. I advised officer Quintan that the officer Xavier wanted the officer on the desk.

Officer Quintan picked up the phone and dialed the phone then handed it to me. I thought he was talking to the officer when he handed me the phone. He called the Lt. Wade and then I advised the Lt. What happened. The Lt. Advised me it was okay. I was following SOP. He would take care of it. When Sgt. Springfield got back on the desk, Officer Quintan asked if we were allowed to give 02's on the air. She stated " We were," and asked what happened? Per Sop we are not allowed to give 02's on the air. After Officer Quintan talked to her, Sgt. Springfield stopped me in the hallway and asked me what happened. When you asked the dispatcher to give the 02's to the Lt. she would tell you "You can not give 02's on the air. Call it in to the desk."

When I tried to tell her she raised a fist with me while talking to me as if she was going to hit me, and two other officers were standing behind her as witnesses to this incident. I just stood there and listened to her talk, when she finished I just walked away. Every time I asked to speak to the Major Ronald via chain of command to try and get out from working for this Bitch because of conflicts of interest, my requests were denied by Sgt. Springfield and Capt. Bourgain.

Boy when there is a click and you are outside of the click you really pay the price for not being one of them. I was called into a closed door meeting between Sgt. Springfield and Capt Bourgain and I was told that "I would not get out from underneath her until I learned to like her and learned to get along with her." My reply to them "was are you done, because as far as I'm concerned this meeting is finished and I don't get along with slut's." One more time I am requesting to speak with the Major," Of course my request was denied.

Now you see part of the reason for the animosity she held towards me was I refused to get along with people who break up happy homes. When someone starts dating someone you know and it breaks up their home and causes problems then how could you get along with this person?

When my Sgt. Realized that she saw me before I ever came to work for her, it was because she was caught walking arm and arm with someone's husband that I knew. Then my troubles became even worse.

I was no good and could do nothing right. It did not matter what I did. She did not like it because she could not break that couple up. When she realized that I was related to those people she really did not like this and she thought that she would make my life a living hell.

I tried every thing I could to get out from under her. My Captain would not allow this because she would take care of his house and animals when he went away. Who knows what else she would take care of as she was known to do that as well? She had such a reputation it is like Anna Nicole Smith and it was to the point that nobody liked her and she was such a witch anyway.

You just never wanted to be around her. As they say its not me she has to answer to, it's her maker and I don't think I would want to be the judgment panel on that one. I will truly leave it up to him. If I never see her for as long as I live it will not hurt my feeling that's for sure.

One occurrence I suppose you could say might be on my side is that they wanted me to go to the Psychological Services when my mother passed away and when this nonsense that didn't stop they told me to call if I needed them. So when this happened, I called and talked to them. They told me to gather about five pens and just start rolling them on the desk, back and forth and shut them out of my mind and that is what I was doing.

When Sgt. Springfield came down from upstairs, she came up to me and practically stood on top of my back saying "If you want my help, all you have to do is say so." I said "I told you, I don't get along with sluts. Excuse me." I guess, people who are supposedly educated don't know when they are not welcomed. When they cause so much trouble and it becomes so detrimental to ones health that they need to be careful. When they go to meet their maker I truly feel sorry for them, as they have a darker side to meet than they know. I said "I think you may have just answered your own statement, I don't want your help. Excuse me."

We were having a Christmas party and I brought in some ice cream from the Dairy Queen and the Major was in the kitchen so he asked why I was so upset? I said: "Sir, I mean no disrespect but I don't want to get any one upset at the party. I have tried to talk to you and I can't get my request in to speak with you. Some how I will figure it out. Let's continue to have a good time at the party. Merry Christmas."

While I was on Vacation my immediate Lt. Hobges came to my part time job and asked me to tell him what was going on. I said " Lt. How much time do you really have?" He said "As much time as you need." The only thing I could tell him was "That if I could not speak to the Major upon returning to work, I would have to take things higher because I could not take any more. I advised the Lt. that my next move would be to the Chiefs office or Internal Revenue to get out from under her. I was on vacation and I was working my part time job and even thou I was working, I was under no stress. I love working at this job. I am very much a people person. I really cannot stand being around a bunch of ASS HOLES , please pardon me and fill in the blanks, as this really upsets me and has tied up my back nerves as I sit here and write this to have to relive this s h T!!

I never imagined that the Department would have been run in such a nonsense way or that I would have stayed where I was if I had a better job. I was working in a Credit Union. I liked where I was working and the people I worked with. They were much nicer. If I were in the same retirement system, I would have transferred back to the Credit Union with no problem, however they are not on the same system. When I started to tell him "what was happening, he could not believe it. I said I was sure you heard it from the other Sgt because all of them talked about the situation as it is continual every day. She does not stop and nobody can get her to stop her nonsense. She thinks that she can do what ever she wants to whom ever she wants and she has another thing coming.

Sue and I are working at the diner and it is a Wednesday it is crazy we are so busy the lines are out the door and around the corner. I have a call party and it is a young actor who comes down to visit his parents. He brings them in to eat here all the time and I know what they want right down to what they drink. I have their ice tea fixed they way they drink it so I put their name on the napkin so when they sit at the table they fell like they are important they get a big kick out of this. Everybody knew that was my table but they never knew who these people were.

During the time when I lost a lot of weight officer Night came to the Station on different occasions saying "Hello" in the hall. Officer Night thought he had the right to put his hands on my ass. I advised him to move it or loose it. I would walk on the treadmill at the station after work in the weight room for an hour and then go home with the other girls. We were allowed to use the equipment so after working until 11:00pm you really didn't want to walk around the block in the dark. At least if it was raining you still got your exercise and you had someone to talk to.

# CHAPTER 3

I WAS WORKING AT the desk at the Doal station when this gentleman walked up to the window and said "He needed to write a report." I said "Okay, how can I help you?" His reply was, "I'm from waste management and I have fifty tags missing and they have to be reported stolen". I asked "Do you have a list of these tags and a contact number so I can call you with a list of case numbers so I can let you know when you can come and pick them up a cover sheet of the page and what you need for the tag agency to obtain new ones for the vehicles."

I informed my Sgt. that fifty tags was being reported missing and that I would call automated systems and see how they wanted to handle entering them into the system. I ran all fifty tags into the computer for ownership information and made copies for the report and for automated system in order to speed up the process.

When I finished I advised my Sgt. I was going to walk the report over to Automated Systems. Upon returning back to my station my boyfriend had called me on the Broward line and did not say who he was but just asked if I was there and when she said "I would be right back," and he would not give his name, she didn't like it. She slammed the phone down on the desk and then put it on hold. He called back a few minutes later and I picked up the phone. He asked me "Who was that?" I said "Honey, I told you that this is the Bitch I told you about."

I was going to my sister's house a few days later and when she saw me in the area, she followed me until I got into the door of her house. My sister asked me "Who was that?" When I told her, she could not believe it." She said "What was she doing following you around here? Why does she know where I live?" I said "I don't think she put it together that it was your house just yet but just the fact that she saw me in this neighborhood she thought she had to follow me to where I was going was enough.

I can't say anything because no one will listen. My captain won't and they will not let me speak to the Major. You know that she and the Captain both live around the corner from you don't you?" She said "No I didn't know that and that's just great." I said "I know honey after all the trouble the two of them caused you they deserve each other but not to be in your back yard."

I am at work and I am receiving a call, when I pick it up it happens to be Officer Night and he is making several of his lewd statements as of when was he going to get a chance with me .That my boyfriend must be fucking lucky to have me . I tried to ignore him but the calls kept on coming. Upon returning from vacation, I put a transfer request in to the Hams Station to work the front desk operations. Officer Night would continually call and say "My boy friend must be fucking lucky that he could have me when ever he wants, do whatever he wants to and he can get a piece of me whenever he wants to."

I am at the front desk and a lady came in asking if she could sign up to ride with an officer. She said she was Officer Rodriguez's cousin. You had to sign a paper saying you wanted to ride with an officer and that the county was not responsible if you got hurt, because you were not allowed to get out of the vehicle unless you went to lunch or the lavatory. You had to have a background check run on you and a number must be issued for you in order to ride. It must be approved by the major of the station. I ran her and did all the final paperwork.

Well, oh my goodness, here comes a warrant in the system with an a/k/a name. I called her by the a.k.a. name she used on the warrant and she answered me so I knew I had the right person. I went oh no. I took the paperwork over to the officer on the desk, with other paperwork and said to the Officer Gooday remember that hit you asked me for earlier today that you were looking for?

She looked at me. I further said "Yes it came in just a few minutes ago for some reason in the middle of my paperwork with hers. You know how these things are. "I then told her" I was going to call the officer at home and advise him so he would not hear it through the grapevine. "See if he could come get her car as to not have it towed out of the parking lot. Then we went over to her and told her what happened, and had her call her husband. She thanked me for handling it that way rather than making a fuss and commotion about it making her a skeptical of the station." Shit happens. The officer came in and took care of the car so it was not there and no questions were asked. While in the Doal Station our Justice System changed computer systems, and I was told I would train the station police officers how to work the new system. I was made to go to classes so that I could teach the officers. I am not a sworn personnel and it is very difficult because they feel they don't have to listen to you.

I made up packages as if they were all sitting in front of there own little screens so that when I went through each screen they could understand how to get to that section. I showed them how to get what they needed out of the system. Making these screens and giving them to the officers so they could follow them as I was showing them made it a lot easier for both the officers and myself while I was teaching them. It was as if they were all sitting in front of there own little computers and entering there screens like I was while teaching them.

However, because we were not in a class room environment with computers I made the next best thing, paper computers. Yet when my co-heart Heather had to teach others how to get into the computers, she adapted the use of these packages, amazing. I don't care that she would use these packages, but yet I'm still on the bad list.

It would be funny if you thought that my Sgt., Fieldgreen, would put herself in a class with me teaching her. She was placed in a class to teach others. This is no problem I would not want to teach her anyway. Of course then they are suppose to learn the rules and regulations, for the State Department of Law Enforcement and have to pass tests which we all understand, however if you don't know how to get what you need what will the benefit be and what good are all the rules and regulations to anyone?

I showed them files that helped them in their investigations and how to run tags and other information that became extremely helpful to them. Making these little packages like little computer screens were very helpful in teaching because it helped them to learn a lot easier and gave them an inside and as it was their own personal property they could take it with them for future reference.

Of course you have the ones that don't want to learn from a civilian. So I would say to them "If you think you can not learn something from me, please don't waste my time or the other parties in the class since that is really what you are suppose to be hereto do learn, so if you don't want to be here you can take the material and go about your way, but I will not make sure you pass your test. You will have a test at the end of this class per SDLE and if you do not pass, you will not be allowed to run subject checks on the computer and it is strictly determined by SDLE not me.

It is be mandated by SDLE not me and if there is any questions or trouble with your passwords you will have to go through me and Kerry in order to get it reset. As you have to be re-certified and take a test every two years anyway. It can be an open book test or closed book it doesn't matter. That is up to the instructor. I usually gave the class the option.

Now I have my third home and it is on Hood St. I cut the grass as part of my exercise program. This would take the anger and frustration out of me. I would be out cutting the grass and my neighbor would send her kids over to help me. I was out cutting the yard one day and they help me pull the weeds off the fence and from the yard. We were trying to cut this bamboo tree down and it became the tree from hell the real nightmare. It just would not die. I told the kids from the beginning that I could not pay them with money, but I could do something else.

We finally got the tree down and then the hedges and brought everything to the front yard. My sister would give me Ice cream from her Ice Cream store so I would give that to the kids for helping me. We became like a neighborhood family. When I first bought this house, it literally had holes in the walls. There was a wall unit air conditioner in the living room that was taken out and the hole in the wall was never covered up.

They left the whole open with comics from the newspaper plastered in the hole. I had sixteen jalousie windows in the house that had to be replaced. The front door needed to be replaced as well. There was an exit in the living room that led to the backyard that they put a jalousie window in. They blocked up the bottom of the house to cover the rest of the cracks, wherever they were.

Of course it needed a paint job inside and out. Then it looked like a forest outside. You had to pull up all these little trees and weeds so that I was not afraid, that I was not going to get attacked when I got home at night. Then I put a little utility room out by the carport so that the lawnmower, yard tools, bike and other little things could be stored outside.

Then I put the kitchen floor down and the appliances in. Then the new furniture, boy is this exciting. My living room is very long. My father helped me make a small bedroom off the living room. I drew up the plans and took them down to the city where they were approved and he put the room in for me.

I placed a deck in the back yard and put a Jacuzzi tub in it. It was sixteen by sixteen. I had ceramic flamingos on the deck and a few chairs. Then I put up a few candles on stands around the Jacuzzi tub to make the atmosphere light up nicer. My girlfriend Lou and her two children were living with me at the time. They had been with me for about five years. She would live with me on and off for a while. This time it was the longest.

We were always there for each other so I never minded the kids and her being there. I really can't remember a time not living without them. They were always a part of my life and will always be a part of my life. I was there when she was pregnant with her daughter. I would take her to the clinic and we would have to sit there for hours. I didn't mind it because, I would be working on her baby gift. I made her an embroidered blanket. When she was done at the clinic, I would take her back home and she would sleep and I would put it under the couch when I heard her wake up. When her son was born, I made him a quilt from scratch. He brought it to school for show and tell and some one at school stole it from him. I felt so sorry for him because he loved his blankie. So I made him a new one every year for Christmas after that until this year when my Arthritis froze my hands up. Besides, who else would put all the love in this blanket for him that I did?

We would have dinner together all the time. I would cook or she would. I would cook a special dinner which became the neighborhood dinner. I used to make Chicken Stir Fry over Wild Rice with vegetables and corn muffins with Honey dates on Sunday after cutting the yard. The kids loved this and then we would watch movies at my house. I would have maybe 17 kids at my house and not one of them was mine. It started off with me making dinner and them doing the dishes then we would watch the movies.

My girlfriend's daughter would get upset with me and tell me that I was not her mother and she did not have to listen to me. She did not like this because I would ask her to leave me a phone number where she was going so if something happened I could call her and get in touch with her or if something happened to her so some one could get in touch with me. One day while in the front yard she got so mad at me that I said to her "I want a number where you are going or you will not go.

You can go back into the house and clean your room and stay with your brother. If you can not leave me a phone number, it is only for your protection and while you are under my roof, when your mother leaves for work you will stay here. That way if something should happen to you, and I then would be held responsible for you I will know who to call and where your mother is."

She said "you don't need to act like my mom, and started to walk off." I said "Gabby, leave me a phone number. That's all you have to do." I went to hand her the paper and pen so she could write the number and name of the party to contact, she said "don't touch me". So I touched her on the arm. I said "Oh you're melting, I touched you." You must be made out of sugar and water because I am touching you and you are melting." You will fall apart in my front yard because I touched you. I guess because of this you cannot leave me a phone number. Her brother told her to just leave the phone number and she could go to her friends house that there would be no problem.

He understood the reason for this that if something happened that I just wanted to be able to get a hold of her in case of and emergency. She just did not like this at all. My neighbors were watching me and they were laughing and she did not like this at all." She remembers this and now thanks me and says that this brought more character to her for she now can appreciate why I was asking for the numbers. Her friends all got into trouble and she is a well respected young lady.

Some times we would do a Barbeque at my neighbor's house and have a party. I would be there to help her clean up the next morning because it wasn't right to leave it for her to do all the cleaning. Of course we all pitched in with the expense. That was not even discussed. One day the guys were all watching football and I was joking around with them saying "well I hope your team wins, but your poor team lost, so I'm going up to the 7'11 to go get a soda and go for the walk. One of the guys wanted to go for a walk with me, so he left because his team was getting a licking in the game. We just started talking and he was telling me how much the kids really admired me and thought of me as their neighborhood mom.

One day I came home from work and my whole house was cleaned up with a note on my bed and flowers from the kids saying "With love to our neighborhood "Mom" we love you."

My girlfriends' young daughter came up to me and asked me "If I could make a couple of dozen cup cakes for a school project for her. I told her, "I would help her make them." Her mom said "She would buy all the ingredients. She knew I usually made my frosting from scratch." I said "Okay, Kit." Kit came over and we made two dozen cup cakes and we were letting them cool off so we went outside for a few minutes. When we got back in B.J., the dog ate about half of the first dozen chocolate cup cakes. Oh my goodness. You could imagine that

HE stayed in the cage and out side for walks quite often for a couple of days after that.

The Kids and I with B.J. would go for rides in the car . You had to take him along or he would get so mad. He would sit in the front passenger seat while you were driving and when the car would stop he would climb into my lap and when the lights were green he would go back into the passenger seat and sit and watch out the passenger window as if he were a little kid. This dog thought he was a little human being.

He did not think of himself as a dog. In our house I got a little cardboard box and cut the side of it down so I could put his toys in it. I would put his toys in the box and tell him to go get them. He was not to sure about the box at first but then warmed up to it. Then I started to teach him to bring his toys back to the box. He was very smart. What a great dog. I truly miss him. I cut the top of the box over and the side down so that it was covered and if he wanted to crawl into it he could. He was a small dog. But none the less very smart.

He knew when I was going out because if I had my keys in my hand he was at my side to go with me as if he was going for a ride as well. Sometimes I had to take him for a ride around the block and that would satisfy him and then back into the house. He didn't care as long as he was in the car for a while he was happy. He was a Boston terrier. He had Beautiful markings. You could not come into the house and say hello to me if I was sitting on the couch without saying hello to him first. Because he felt like he was part of the family as well. He wanted his attention too. If he didn't get his attention he would get up on the back of the couch and sit there before you could say hello to me. He was unreal.

We were getting ready to leave the drive way and he was in my lap with his paws on the steering wheel and looking back at the kids, as if he were saying " Are you ready to go?" When I told him to get in his seat, he jumped in the passenger's seat and looked out the window. He was such a smart little fellow and the kids all loved him.

# CHAPTER 9

MY GIRLFRIEND AND THE kids lived with me for many years. One of us was always at the house with the kids. We have been friends since the 70's. One night Bob came over and I told Pep her son that Bob was coming over, so if he came in when I was in the shower not to get worried because he had a key to my house. When I got out Bob had not gotten there yet. When Bob arrived I went to introduce him to Pep, he said "Hi Bob from FPL." Bob said "Hi, But what do you mean?" He said "You know, the Bob you always hear about but never see." Bob said "You got me there." You always hear me but never see me. You are probably right. Now you can't say that anymore" We laughed so hard over this.

On several occasions officers would come up to you and ask you to run information in the system for whatever reason. Sometimes it for there own personal use and sometimes it was for investigations. Sometimes it was because they might not know how to get what they are looking for or maybe they are looking for something and they don't have the time to finish, so they will have you do the rest. Or they just don't have the clearance to get in the series of investigations. Maybe they are rookies and are not certified to run subjects yet or just don't know how.

Maybe they just did not want to learn how to work the computer so they would ask you to run the information in the computer and get it for them. There was this one officer who was always in trouble and was on the desk because he could not stay away from his girlfriend's house.

He still had his gun and badge imagines that and he was on the desk and still had clearance to run information in the computer.

I was standing in the roll call room cleaning the board when one of the Sergeants came up to me and gave me a kiss on the shoulder and said "Hello kid, your looking great keep up the good work. By the way I have the tape back from the graduation ceremonies would you like to see to see them?" I said "Sure, but please for your sake and mine, please watch what happens because I have a witch on my back." He said "Don't worry I will take care of it. " I said "Thank you". I left it alone. After work I went on the treadmill like usual and of course there was trouble because I watched the tape. I got called into the office and told it was none of my business and I should only mind my own business.

I responded with I was asked by the sergeant if I wanted to watch the tape and I wasn't hurting anyone. It was just my Sgt's noisy way of being in my business. She would boss any one around she thought she could. She would also sleep around with anyone and everyone that she knew and is the God honest truth. She could care less whose marriage she broke up. She was dating a detective once and was told to "Stay out of the General Investigations Unit during working hours" because it caused too much trouble.

Sgt. SpringField called me in the Sgt. Office and said "In a meeting at which I was standing against the wall with my arms crossed and she went to grab them." Then she said yelling at me "You can ask Sgt. Frane because she did not like that he talked to me or that he respected me or even would meet me for coffee to listen to the nonsense she was putting me through." The other Sgt's knew of it as well, yet no one could or would do anything about it. No one had any backbone to stand up to her to do anything. If Sgt Frane wanted me to go for coffee to talk to me it was none of her dam business. She did not like the fact that he would take the time to talk to me at all. She wanted him to date someone else at the department so he was not allowed to talk to me.

Just to get her goat one day, he came up to the desk and asked me in front of all the other people if I had anything for dinner? I said "I forgot dinner because I was in a hurry today so I will have to go get something." The Sgt's said "They were going to Wendy's and would I like them to pick up something for me?" I said "That would be nice, how about a piece of chicken breast, a baked potato with butter and a salad. I will pay for that now. They said "No wait until we get back and we will give you a receipt so you will know how much it is." I said "okay, thank you." Of course Sgt Springfield did not like this one bit as she did not like me talking to him in the least.

When Sgt Frane would bring me dinner, I would insist on paying because I did not want the problems from my Sgt. He told me that he could afford it and I said "I'm sure you could but it's not a matter of money, it's a matter of getting in trouble because you want to buy me lunch." He said "Again I will take care of that." If anyone else came to the station to take me out she did not like it especially if it were a gentlemen. Bob never came there because he did not want to see her because he would have put her in her place.

I was riding my bike on the weekend and it truly was a beautiful day and as I was riding I hit a bump in the sidewalk causing me to literally put the bike pedal in my knee. I was trying to get back home and as this was not the age of cell phones, so as I tried to pedal home, I lost more and more blood by the minute. Every time I tried to pedal the bike it shot out like a hose spitting out and by the time I got to my house I was covered in blood. It looked like something out of a horror movie. My neighbor couldn't believe what had happened and had to take me to the hospital. I had to have seven stitches in my knee and wound up on churches.

Oh boy here we go again what will my Sgt
have to say about this one ????????????

# PART B
# CHAPTER 10

WHEN I HAD TO go to work and had to finger print people it was obvious I wasn't able to stand on churches and do that so one of the public service aides worked the desk with me to help me until I got the stitches out and was able to walk again however, my Sgt had things to say about me being on churches.

I am a firm believer that she will have to meet her maker one day and answer for all her troubles she causes on this earth. She has caused her share and more. I honestly don't know how she sleeps at night. You will not only answer for what you do not in this world buy truly in the next. My Public service aide could not believe her when she said "I was just looking for attention." She said "I don't think so. I certainly wouldn't have put a bike pedal in my knee for that."

I asked her if she wanted the emergency room records just to shut her up. When I got to the emergency room, one of the guys that I know was working off duty there and saw me he took me in the emergency room and asked "what happened?" I said "I was ridding my bike and I hit a bump then the next thing I knew the pedal was in my knee and I had to get it out and get home in order for fire rescue to help. I called a girlfriend to come and pick me up and bring me to the hospital. I told her not to look at it just to driver me to the hospital emergency room and get an attendant to come out and get me as it was bleeding real bad. I could not walk on it or it would just start bleeding again.

Fire rescue bandaged it up tight enough to send me to the hospital but told me that I needed stitches so I had to go to the hospital because they do not stitch up wounds. When we got to the hospital my friend went inside and got the attendant and they came out and got me and took me in and started working on my knee. They of course gave me a tetanus shot and of course they do not tickle. They asked me if I had a way to get back home and I said "My girlfriend brought me here and I have to call her and she will pick me up when I am done."

They had to clean out the road rash with a brush and let me tell you that did not tickle. If you ever have to go through that it hurts !!!!!!!!!

I was working at the Department from 3 pm till 11 pm then I would work the diner from midnight until six or seven in the morning and woke up at 12 noon. I would get a wake up call from a gentleman friend that I met at Denny's. He would call me at noon every day and tell me that this was my wake up call. I would call him when I got to the station, and he would come see me at Denny's. Then he would spend time with me on my days off. He had a young son and one day they came over, he sat on the couch and he was so tired he fell asleep. I didn't have any toys in the house, so I told his son we had a mission.

His mission, if he accepted was "To ask dad if he could go for a ride to the grocery store to get something for dinner." Should he accept this mission we would go get diner. There was a toy store next door. I gave him twenty dollars and I told him "He could buy what ever twenty dollars worth of toys twenty dollars would buy, so he would have something to play with when he came over to play at my house." Then I asked him "Is that fair?"

Bob never told me that he was seeing other people until I went up there to spend time with him after my mom died. I thought I was pregnant by him which I was so happy about having a child with Bob that would have made me very happy after being with him for so long. Then he told me that some other woman tried that on him in South Carolina, and I said "excuse me what are you talking about?" He said "she said she thought she was pregnant but she could not be because I cannot have children because I had a vasectomy ten years ago." I said "how come you never told me this? Didn't you think this was important enough for me to know this?" " I should have been able to make this decision for my self as to whether I wanted to be in such a relationship, as to not being able to have kids or not with someone.

I was so mad "I told him to put my bags back in the car and I would go back the next morning as I did not want to be with such a deceitful person." He said "what do you mean?" I said "you should have told me ten years ago you could not have kids." He said "you never asked." I said "I should not have had to ask that question." When I got back home of course like any girlfriend I called Lou and we talked for hours, I was so upset. She could not believe it.

She asked "what are you going to do?" I said "I don't know. You know I just started to see someone else and now that Bob pulled this number on me. I think it will be easier to let him go." She said "I think your right. Even though you guys have been together for a while it will be hard but probably the best thing." Bob and I didn't see each other for such a long time.

Bob was still living in South Carolina at the time and this gentleman and I were just friends. When his son came over I did not think it was fair that he would have to just sit and color or watch a movie that was not meant for him to watch, if it was to scary for him. I had a big house so he could go in the backroom and play with his toys. If he got tired he could always take a nap in the spare bedroom. He knew this and was welcome to do so if he wanted to.

One day his dad said he had to go do a job and could he leave him with me? I said "Of course that was not even a question. When you get back we will still be here. Don't worry." He said "I'll call when I'm on my way home and we can go out to dinner. Would that be okay with you? I mean you have had him all day." I said "Don't be silly. He's no trouble. If you are too tired, I'll make dinner. Just pick up something you might like and I will make it." Call me later and we will decide later.

I was driving down the road and there is this guy driving next to me. He is not bad looking if I might say. He is making these gestures for me to pull off the highway and go to the gas station. I have never done such a thing but I thought, why not what is the harm? It is a public place and I can always get gas anyway. I pulled over and I started talking to him. He asked me for my phone number and I said "Okay, I gave my number to him and we started talking on the phone." He asked me if we could go out. I told him that I thought that I would like that some time. We went out to dinner and a movie. He asked to see me again. I said I would like that. We started to see one another. Bob and I were four states apart and I had no idea that he was seeing other women. This was the only person I was just starting to see.

All of a sudden Bob was at my door and I had no idea that he was even in the state. The gentleman said "I am not going to put up with this, and walked out and I never heard from him again." I truly wish this would of not happened as I would have liked to have further dated him and gotten to know him. Who knows what might have come of that relationship.

Now while at the Doal station there was an individual who asked me out (Frane) and I wanted to go, however when Springfield found out my life was made a living hell. If any guy came to the desk and started talking to me she would have a fit, especially if it were someone she wanted to date. She was dating someone from the detective bureau and this person was married, which needless to say caused problems when his wife, when she came to the station and she was there. I could not ask this detective to come to the desk to answer a phone call or see a victim without her getting upset. I have only two more years before I'm on a ten year retirement with the county, I need to try and stick this out.

I applied to become a police officer and I passed the dry shooting tests and the Scenarios that they gave you to do. After all I do write the reports at the Station and have picked up quite a bit of information from being around the station and the officers. I would have to read the officers reports when I typed the incident log in the morning so I would also get additional information from this source. All of a sudden my hands were swollen like baseballs, and my Arthritis doctor told me I better stop shooting because is was going to destroy my hands.

I told the Doctor that I went out and did try some shooting at the department in order to become a police officer. And he told me that I could not do that line of work.

I talked to my brother in law and asked him what the best thing was for me to do because I did not want to get taken off the department because of this, so he informed me to withdraw my application for personal reasons. At this time, and they would not hold it against me nor would they be able to take me off the department because of medical reasons. I passed all the test they had given me, the dry shooting, the written test and psychological test.

Well my transfer request finally came in for the Hamm station. I hope the shit will stop here, the year is now 1991. This is a new station and a new start for me I really hope so. I helped set up the front desk and the files, and operations, and the fleet vehicles. I assisted the armory in setting up the vehicle files and getting the fleet vehicles ready for the opening of the station.

We are starting off with five Police Record Specialists. Three PRS are on days and two on afternoon shift. That's the way it supposes to be. This is a heavy Spanish speaking district. I don't speak Spanish neither does the officer on the desk. We are not supposed to enter subpoenas into the system. Well guess what we were required to do just that. We were to fingerprint people, write reports, answer phones, help officers, teach officers, assist the public, and make tow truck identification cards.

We were also to run background checks on people which are called clearance letters for apartments so they can get approval for the new place to live. Don't you think that such a thing is against ones constitutional rights, you have the right to live anywhere and you should not have to have a clearance letter from the local police department in order to get an apartment, a condominium, or any place to live. So even if you are buying a town house they want you to get such a letter. You are buying a house and this is expected of you. Is this something you think is right that you have to have just to purchase your home? I really don't I feel it is a void in my constitutional rights.

Now it's time to do the Tow Truck Identification Cards. I would get about eight of them at a time. So, I called the company and spoke to the owner and said (We will call her Terry) "Terry, could you get all the guys Drivers licenses together and copy them on light and fax them over to the station to me so I can get a head start on the paperwork." "This way I can retype the fingerprint cards, get the paper work typed, run all the drivers licenses and ready for laminating except pictures, then take prints when the guys come in. Well, then I'm thinking, if this is done every year and there is nothing different, why can't they just put a sticker on the back of the previous one like the drivers licenses and save all this redundant paperwork? How much would it save the county? So I did the study and put it through and I saved the county a lot of money and I received a commendation for this.

I would continually teach Louise how to do this work but it just was not her cup of tea, so to say, and she had a hard time getting it down. I would have to do it over and over, which after a while can get on your nerves if you know what I mean.

I would give Terry a heads up so to say if one of her drivers had a warrant or if they were not able to be going to go back to work. If they needed to have someone drive them in and she respected that and always had her husband who also owned the company, drive that driver in. Then I did their ID'S and the midnight dispatcher last so it was fast. Needless to say my drivers did not spend much time off the road when they came in to get there new ID cards, the loss of time off the road were real minimal.

I am still receiving phone calls from officer Night asking me "when he can have a piece of me and saying that my boyfriend must be fucking lucky that he can have me any time he wishes. He can have me any way he wants whenever he wants to." I cannot stand to hear this person on the phone. At this point I really want to throw up, for some reason Officer Night has shown up in the station and I hope he does not see me. I am truly doing my best not to see him. I am hiding. I will let Arter know what is going on later.

Once again I was appointed to teach the station personnel the Justice system on the computer and I had to teach the personnel how to work the front desk. I had to teach them how to write reports and fingerprint people. There are supposed to be Two Police Record Specialists on the desk. There is currently one PRS and one Officer and we have to pull a Public Service Aide from the road to speak Spanish as none of us do. We are currently printing civilians from 7am to 6pm.

When the afternoon PRS comes in to work she is suppose to relieve me on the desk and start the duties of the desk. If there is someone in the lobby that needs to be fingerprinted or needs a report written she should attend to that person so as not to make me go on overtime to have to handle the call if it were a report. When she comes in she puts her belongings down and goes upstairs or goes over to the officers and starts talking to them but will not start handling the front desk.

I have brought this up to the Sgt's attention but again nothing happens. She would braid the officer's hair that was working on the desk so that it was above the collar length instead of the officer pinning it up before that particular officer shift starts. It was not necessary for her to do this as that was not her job. If she wanted to do this she should have been on her break or when it was a slow period, not at shift change, or when there were people in the lobby. She just did this so that she did not have to be on the desk when I was there. I did nothing to her she just would not stay on the desk. I went upstairs to get the mail as this was one of my morning duties, and she had a letter from some place. I placed it on the desk and asked the Sgt to give it to her so that it would not cause any problems.

She told him that I did not have the right to bring it down stairs and that I had a Federal offense against me because I was handling her mail. He told her that I was the mail carrier for the desk and she was incorrect so that I did nothing wrong and to stop her non-sense or he would right her up. That she was carrying things a little too far and all I did was to bring the mail down to the desk and ask him to give it to her to prevent an issue, because as I knew it would cause a problem in her mind. She did not like this too well and did not take it any further.

Today there is this lady that looks extremely nice in the lobby. Arter said to me "Lee-Ann, could you do me a big favor and find out what she needed." When a female comes into the lobby that looks like that, the guys act like they have never seen a female before, and there tongues are hanging out of their mouths and they act like a bunch of hot dogs which is discussing. I would say to them "Can't you act like you have some manners and not stare at this young lady. Go put your tongues back in your mouth and act like professional people not like children that has never seen a girl before. This is why Arter did not want to be in the room with her alone, so he asked me to be in there with him when he took the report so nothing could happened. I said "No problem I would do that for him."

Arter is the most wonderful person you would want to meet. It is not fair that the officer on the desk be left alone to work the desk and I would not appreciate it myself, so I will not do it to him. However we have to work 8 ½ hr days to accommodate a lunch break, if the other PRS who is suppose to come down and relieve me doesn't come down, then I am stuck there. While I'm on the desk at the Hamm districts I keep receiving these phone calls from an Officer Night about when is he going to have a piece of me? The whole department has to go to sexual harassment classes and I asked the Lt Hickleberry "how could I make sure that I am not in the same class with a certain officer on the department" Her reply was "I'll be right back."

Officer Arter, myself and other officers were at the desk as it was shift change when officer Night came in and he told me to wheel myself across the desk to him. I asked him if there was something that someone else could get him as I was on crutches and it was not possible for me to get anyone any thing. Officer Arter told me that he thought it was time for me to leave before I got hurt when shift change came in so he walked me out. He asked me if I was okay. I said "yes and I will talk to you in the morning." I said "Arter please keep him away from me". He said "I will keep him away from you kid is there something I should know?" I said "Can I tell you in the morning or do you need to know now? I want to get out of here before he comes back out here. I don't want him following me or catching up with me to ask me to meet with him." He said "I could tell him in the morning." I said "Okay I will tell you in the morning I promise. Can we go for coffee and talk outside the station or when it is quite and there is no around?" The next morning I told Arter what it was all about. He said "He could not believe that I had to go through this and that this Officer should be made to pay for what he did."

I thought the Lieutenant was going to see about the class schedules, but that was not the case, she advised me that I had a 10:00 am appointment in internal review and I would be driven by a female officer and that she would pick me up, when I was finished she would bring me back to the station. I asked my friend Officer Arter to step outside, and I told him what was going on, he said "I would have never known what was going on, you know you could have come to me a long time a go." I said "I know I didn't want to put you in that position."

He said "That explains his actions to you the other day at the front desk, and why you wanted to leave. "When I got back from the internal review the outcome was that he was not allowed to talk to me and he was not allowed to call to me. If he called the station, it had to be reference to a police matter only. If I answered the phone, he was to discuss police work solely. He was not to go by my house or call my house. He was not to go to my off duty job. He was not to transfer to the station where I worked at. If he called me and continued to harass me then he will loose his gun and badge.

This could not protect me as, it is just a double standard to me. How could you say it protects when someone else would be arrested for that very same action? I am still working at the Hamm District and for some reason, when I go to get into my car and start it up the car will not start. I have just worked two shifts and it is late at night. I called triple A for a tow and it was the towing company that I do the ID cards for in the day shift.

# CHAPTER 11

WHEN THEY FOUND OUT it was me, the boss said "take her where she has to go and make sure she is safe. Do not leave her if she does not have a way to get home as it is one in the morning." I called the dealer in the morning to see if they could find out what was wrong with the car as it was under warranty, and they said "someone put sugar in my gas tank." I had to make a police report and have the gas tank dropped and cleaned and blown out. I thought the problem was taken care of. About a week later approximately four o'clock in the afternoon I went to go home from work and I again could not get the car started.

I called for a tow and the guys towed it to the dealer. They dropped the tank again and said "they must have not gotten all the sugar out of the gas line." I said "I don't think you fixed it correctly the first time so now I am back here again and I have the same problem. Please fix the car or if you can't then give me a new one and lemon law this one." I will call the insurance company and get them involved in this case immediately." I called the insurance company and had them come out to check the car and they said "Because I had a police report and it was sugar in the tank that it had to be taken care of immediately." I said "Thank you , fix my car or I will take this matter to the insurance commissioner." It was not my fault that someone put sugar in my tank and that I cannot get the vehicle fixed, however I cannot be stranded on the side of the road as I am handicapped.

Oh boy, now here comes Hurricane Andrew. We are all working 12 hr shifts ad required. I'm like all others, getting up and getting ready for work, taking the dog out to do her business and feed her. Well I slipped and fell and broke my ankle, broke that's an understatement. I destroyed it. I turned it 180 degrees backwards and when I looked down and saw it I literally freaked out.

I could not remember who to call at this point because I went into shock. I remember that I pulled the phone down and start dialing a number, it just happened to be the station where I worked. I told the girl on the phone please do not hang up the line because I did not know what number I called. Then I asked "Her to call my sister and ask her to have her come and get me and take me to the hospital because I think I broke my ankle."

Then I said "I think you better put me in the sick log." She said "What do you mean you think you broke your foot?" I said "Well, it's turned all the way around, my toes are behind me, and my heel is in front." When she told the Lieutenant he told her to call Fire Rescue and send them to my house, and then call my sister. By the time Fire Rescue got to my home I had the nerve to turn my foot back forward.

I thought that if it was not turned back soon that I could possibly lose my foot. My dog was sitting next to me and would not leave my side. Then she got back on the phone and asked me "If I saw lights yet," I said "No, what kind of lights was I suppose to see? I wasn't even aware that she called Rescue." Fire Rescue had to stand my dog's cage back up in the kitchen, so I could get her to go into it, so that they could attend to me. She went into the cage and sat there like a good little girl. They then took me to the hospital.

At this point one of my co-workers showed up at my house after she heard that I broke my foot, and wanted to take me to the hospital. Fire Rescue said "She could meet me there and then she could call my family." I spent three hours in the emergency room and they told me that "I would have to have surgery." Which would consist of having seven pins and a plate put in my ankle.

I asked the doctor for a second opinion because I was scared because of what they told me. They tried to set my foot five times that morning and it would not stay. I could not take any more of them pulling on my foot and having to set it, so the doctor on call told them after the x-rays were taken to set it in a splint and send me to the office and we would discuss the next course of action. I told the nurse that was taking my x-ray that there was a problem while he was taking it that I did not want him touching me anymore.

The head nurse told him to go into the next room and she would take it herself. Then she told him that he should go home because he should not argue with a trauma patient in reference to the needs of the patient. I had 75mg of Demerol and I still felt the pain from them trying to set my foot back that morning.

The doctor on call just happened to be the orthopedic doctor I had for years, after the nurse told me his name I was somewhat relieved, that it was "Doctor Druck " the nurse came back and then said he wants us to set your foot and send you over to his office, "I said okay." I then went to his office and he examined the X-rays. He came back and tried to set my foot again but to no avail, and then said to me "Listen kid, we have tried to set your foot several times this morning both here in the office and at the hospital and it is not going to stay." I said "Okay, Doctor Druck this is your field not mine, in your medical opinion, what is the best move?"

He then said "I am suggesting that you have the surgery to set this foot straight. It will require having the seven pins and a plate surgically implanted in your foot that they told you about at the hospital, and you will be off your foot for about a week maybe two I can not tell you how long the surgery will last it depends on how long it takes while we are in there." I then said "When is the best time." He said "See you tomorrow morning at 6:00 am." I said "I will be at the hospital at 6:00 in the morning." My sister took me to the hospital and stayed with me until the time I was to go under surgery. I spent the next five and a half hours in surgery. They told my sisters that I had complications in surgery because of the damage that I did. I turned my foot completely backwards and that did more damage than they expected so they had to do more recovery.

Tara came over to my house and spent the first week with there, while I was in the hospital, so she could take care of the dog. I had to learn to walk on a set of crutches and walk up a flight of stairs because stairs were in my townhouse. I was allowed to go home after a week of bed rest. My first exercise was to put my foot down on the side of the bed. I told the doctor, "piece of cake." He said "okay, go ahead." I said "Oh Shit man that hurt." I thought I was going to kill somebody. It hurt like the devil. He just laughed. Then he said "it will be a lot easier from hear on out, I promise you. Kid" I said "I hope so."

After being released from the hospital I was placed on strict bed rest for another two weeks in my home. I was aloud to return to work only after my foot was in a hard cast, so that no one would be able to hit it or damage the procedure. I was allowed to be on a light duty status. I was on crutches for 20 weeks non weight bearing and 20 weeks soft cast learning to walk with therapy. After the 40 weeks of being in the two different types of casts, I had to have the pins removed because my foot rejected them.

Of course this didn't set well with the Department. I was written up with an unsatisfactory attendance, when for during the 13 years I was there I had never used as much as a sick day like I have had to now. I do not feel this was fair to me. When I broke my foot, my doctor told me no driving. Okay, I'll go along with that. Yet when the doctor said "NO" driving, how am I going to get to work, since I live alone. We were working 12 hour shifts and as I asked if one of our Public Service Aides could pick me up, their reply "Was of course, NO, no one gets special treatment." When I was in the hospital, Tara would come up to the hospital at night after work and see me and if I needed anything she would bring it to me. Such as , if I needed a book or any crocheting she would bring it to me.

I asked again, "What if I got a ride from a PSA from the district where I live into the next district to the area of the Hamm to the station?" There is something you must realize here the distance to my job was through 2 counties and I had to travel a very dangerous stretch of road know as highway 27 or alligator alley. Now this stretch of road is considered dangerous, due to the fact that many accidents occur and it is close to the everglades.

Of course to make it difficult on me their answer was again "NO." So I didn't ask any more. So I did the next best thing that I could. I didn't drive with my right foot. Now I could not do this as I had a white hard cast on my leg, I sat in the driver seat, pushed the seat back, placed my right leg on the passenger's seat of the vehicle then drove my car with a towel over my lap gracefully and carefully. Praying I didn't get in an accident as to not re-break my foot or leg hitting the shift gear on the floor board. Well, guess what, I got into another accident, "dam" I had this awful contusion just above the cast. My doctor was extremely upset that I was driving and I said to him "What other choice do I really have, I cannot get help from my job and I can not take a taxi as it would eat my entire paycheck up, and if that is not a good reason the bus is totally out of the question so please tell me, what do you suggest I do?"

Imagine this in your mind as you are reading this how I would go shopping. I had to push the shopping cart with my chest and catch up to it on my crutches. Then I would have to try and get what I needed and place these items in the cart and push the cart all over again. As the items were placed in the cart it got heavier and impossible at times to push. One of the bag boys saw me doing this and offered to push the shopping cart through out the grocery store for me and then bag the groceries, so they were not so heavy, so I could carry them with my crutches.

Then when I went outside he asked "if I had someone at home to take them in the house?" I said "no I live alone." He said "how are you going to get them in your house?" I said "I don't know I will think of something. Thank you very much for your concern."

When I got home I got a three tier cart and the dog's leash. I put the leash and attached it to the cart and pulled it to the car. Then I put the groceries in the cart and pulled them into the house as I stepped with my crutches. This sometimes would take several trips as I could not put to much weight in the cart because it would be to heavy for me to pull. Well my neighbors thought I was crazy, yet no-one offered to help, so I did what I had to do. This was not easy for me as I was in the non weight bearing cast at the time.

Now here's one for you, my Arthritis doctor broke his ankle during the Hurricane Andrew a few months latter. He was up and doing surgeries on his. He did not break his as bad as I did. He told me that I would have Arthritis in my ankle really bad. I literally would have to deal with some form of arthritis, but he could not tell me of course when or how bad it would hit me. Surprise I have it bad now.

After Hurricane Andrew hit us, the district would receive all kinds of Humanitarian relief and it would come into the back of the station. We received water by the pallets from stores. Diapers came from stores, food from all over. Clothing came from everywhere. Things where dropped off in the lobby of the station from patrons and people struck by the hurricane as well.

The National Guard was sent to our station and relocated to another one once they could get through the streets. When we could, we set up temporary shelves in the back of the station to organize the items that where coming in. We somehow received a very large BBQ pit. Well let me tell you, we were actually barbequing on this large pit and cooking all sorts of things such as chicken, hamburgers, hot dogs, coffee, what ever we could. We made it through with the grace of God. Thank You Lord very much.

We were cooking for the national guard, the officers from different districts and other entities as well. Every body that found out that we had this big pit would get something that was donated and bring it to us so we would cook it to keep the moral going. The devastation was so bad and as we did not have electricity for months, some of the officers lost their homes as well as others in this storm, and were required to work 12 hours shifts as well as the others. They would sleep in the back of the station and you could hear some of them snoring so hard, because they were sleeping on cots. Off course all fingerprinting for civilian purposes was suspended at this time the only thing that was conducted was report writing of legitimate matters. Curfews were strictly enforced due to loitering.

Then came our first Thanksgiving together. We had a lot to be thankful for. We had no fatalities during all of this. We had only minor injuries. So we made our First Annual Thanksgiving Dinner at the Station. I organized this dinner, ordered things from Publix, had enough cooked by Publix and had one of the Sgt's. in the General Investigation Department take me to the store and pick up the dinner and then set it up. It was lovely.

Everybody joined in and all the different units came in off the road. I ordered enough food for them as well and they would take there lunch break and come in and would get a dish, eat and then go back on the road. This was very special due to the type of devastation that we went through. It was enough that it was truly important to have this affair and be very grateful for all we had in friendship at the station as well, as (if you believe in God) then it was his will for us to be together and be in one piece.

Our first arrival of children was starting to be born after the hurricane and at the station. The first born baby into the family of our secretaries was a boy. Well, we had a big shower for her and surprisingly enough due to the devastation of the Hurricane all of the people in the station wanted to join in which was really nice. She got everything she needed for the baby. It became the station baby shower. We had a big luncheon and the guys would come in off the road to join us. They would take turns so that every one could join in. This made it especially nice.

We would continually make dinners in-between the months after the hurricane for the station and officers and the national guardsman that were stationed there with the food that was left. It took several months to clean up the disaster caused by the Hurricane. Well on one particular day, we were cooking this huge pot of food, and someone walked by the stove accidentally turning off the potatoes.

Well the major, who was a female did not see who it was, someone just happened to turn around and see me standing next to the counter, at which I was actually leaning on because I was still on my churches at the time. The major then said to me "" Lee-Ann why did you turn off the potatoes?" I said "I didn't, I'm just leaning because my cast is getting a little heavy. As a matter of fact I need to go sit down because my leg is starting to swell. I'm been up on my leg a little too long. Please excuse me and I'll be back in a few when it simmers down."

When my leg simmered down, I went back in the kitchen and continued to help the girls with the dinner. Don't think for a minute that that didn't cause a problem, that I was supposedly the one to have shut off the potatoes. How childish. Just turn them back on and continue to cook them. It is not as if they would not have continued to cook. She just needed someone to yell at, and it happened to be me of course. I was sitting in the conference room when the Sgt came up to me and asked "If I was okay?" I said "Yes, my foot was just swelling in the cast a little so I had to sit for a while and get off of it because it was bothering me. I'll be okay. But thank you anyway."

# CHAPTER 12

Now I HAD TO have handicap equipment placed in my vehicle as it is necessary to drive with a left foot gas pedal now. When the company placed this equipment in my car it literally got stuck in the floor board and when I went to go around the corner in the parking lot, I went through a concrete wall. I tried to avoid this by going into the dirt field behind this parking lot but I could not.

When the officer came to write the report and take me to the hospital they asked "who placed this equipment in the car?" The company representative would not even talk to him as he said "we need to talk to our lawyers first." The police officer said "I am sending this woman to the hospital and someone is responsible for this, I need to talk to the representative NOW." My car was destroyed and I only had it for three days. I was devastated. They took the car to Toyota and when I got there they could not believe that my car was in such an accident and asked "if I was okay?" It took about three months to get my car fixed and then it still did not run correctly.

As I returned back to work on light duty and as I was assigned to work upstairs doing the pawn shop files, getting them ready to start new files. I wore dresses with pockets so if I needed something I could get it or I would carry a Shopping bag with handles so I could carry it with my crutches. I didn't ask anyone to get things for me because I didn't want to cause any trouble. Nor would they do it anyways. Well at Christmas time my girlfriends were so cute, they went out and bought a big RED Christmas Stocking and put it on my cast with a small bell on my foot. It was cute however my foot was so sensitive from the surgery that I couldn't take and leave it on, so I tied it to my crutches so I could carry what I needed. I still have it, and I enjoyed the joke for it let up some of the tension.

Remember the most recent accident I told you about, well I am in the same car and when I am driving this vehicle, it feels like it wants to jump ahead of me. I took it back to the shop and told the mechanics this and they did not believe me of course. I did not know what I was talking about because I am a woman. Well over the weekend, I was out shopping and while in the parking lot, I went to back the vehicle up out of a parking space and the car skipped causing me to hit something. I thought let me put the car in park and get out and see what I hit. It was only the rear bumper and nothing was damaged so it really was no big deal.

When I got back in the car it jumped again this time I did not move the car at all from out of parking lot yet, and it slipped out of gears and went forward. The next thing I knew it was going and I almost hit another car, so in order to avoid hitting the other car I turned the wheel, my car jumped the sidewalk and went into a building. Man I was so scared I almost shit my draws, I could not get out of the vehicle I was stunned. Someone called the police and fire rescue.

The guys from fire rescue and the towing company moved the car and told me that I could drive the car. But I was shaking so bad that they said "maybe you better not drive the car as you might get into another accident. Where should we tow the vehicle to, so that it can be fixed in the morning?" We took the car to my house and I called Toyota in the morning. When I had them pick the car up, I went with the car and then to the head mechanic, and I said to him "Jose, before anyone touches the car, listen to what I am telling you. I need to know if this could have been the cause of the accident, that I had yesterday and the insurance company is also going to ask the same question."

When I told him what occurred he said after looking at the vehicle up on the racks "that the transmission was cracked and it had a leak in it and I was correct that's why the car was skipping." I was lucky to be alive after going through the building. He said "he would tell this to the insurance adjuster as well." I would have to believe that I just was in the hands of the almighty man above and had him on my side, because trust me going through a building is no fun.

Now while at the Hamm district, I am sitting at the front desk, talking with Lt. Hickleberry and Off Arter. We are talking about the sexual harassment classes we have to go through. I asked her "How can I make sure I do not get scheduled in the same class as a certain officer on the department?" She said "She would be right back "When she returned she told me "That I had a 10:00am appointment in internal review and since I was the victim and I would be transported by a female officer and brought back to the station by the same officer, when I was finished.

Since this meeting I was told the same as before that this Officer would loose his gun and badge if he persists on engaging in this activity. I was sent home for the rest of the day, with three days off.

In 1991 I was injured and lost a lot of time and a certain Lt. would not let up on me or anything I did. This Lt.'s name is Darrel. I would buy coffee for the desk which is paid for by the officers and personnel. I usually get the coffee when I go to the grocery store on my time, and I'm doing my own shopping. In July 1991 on a Monday I was not aware that there was not any coffee at the station.

Then Captain Lerman came down looking for coffee and because we were out, I had to go right then and there to the store to get the coffee, he said "Okay, no problem. One of the officers can take you." As I was getting ready to get into my car, one of the units asked "where I was going?" When I advised them I was going to get coffee for the station, they told me not to use my own vehicle. They advised me that they would take me to the store.

It was only around the corner, but not in walking distance." The officer said "Tell me what you get and give me the money, I'll go get it." I don't want to cause you any kind of problems with the chain of command (ass holes) meaning what they did. As this officer saw just what had happened.

Captain Lerman saw me and said "Oh, good coffee soon!" I said "As soon as it gets here." He said "what do you mean?" Didn't you go get it, I thought I said it was okay for you to go get it?" I said " I started to but I got hollered at so one of the guys he went to get it for me, and as we speak it's at the back door." He said "Who hollered at you?" Officer Arter said "Sir, I'll bring you your coffee and explain." Capt. Lerman said "Okay." Officer Arter after he came back down said I think it will stop for a while, Lee-Ann. I said "I hope so."

Lt. Darrel asked Officer Arter why I had to go to the store to get coffee and was this an everyday occurrence? Other clerical personnel in the station are allowed to go get breakfast without any hassles. Why is this necessary for her to hassle me all the time? I do my share of the work and more so why is this necessary? In January of 91 I received several 911 beeps to the station. Upon calling them back no one could advise me who called.

**When I broke my foot, I had this lady that used to come to the station to sell us Avon. Her name was Amanda, and she was extremely nice to me. She came to my house and brought me my Avon. She also wanted to see if I needed anything or if I needed to go to the store, or if I had a doctor's appointment or anything. When she told me that she was getting out of the business, she said "She would hand over her customers to me at the station and would give me her contacts around if I wanted them." I said "I would take care of the girls at the station so I could get my Avon that way." NOT necessarily to SELL the AVON as a part time job, just so I** could get my stuff I wanted.

And that way the girls could get what they wanted and I never charged them a service charge for their Avon, just the taxes and what it cost. I told them when I was going down there to pick up what I wanted, I would pick up theirs. I thought that was being extra kind and helpful. Now all of a sudden, I am supposed to fill out an outside employment application for selling this Avon. How stupid can they be!!!!. I was not selling Avon. I was doing all of them a favor by picking their Avon up for them. I never made no money on it.

Now as my brother in law made the P.A. president and some people did not like him or this at all. Trust me, some of my problems were made a lot worst because of his new position. What he does should be his business not mine. It should not cause difference to me and vice versa. My brother in law told me that if he made president of the P B A, that I would not be liked even more if certain people found out I was connected (Sister in Law) to him, and it became very true as you will see.

During this time period, while on the desk, we have several desk drawers assigned to each shift. I keep all necessary paperwork in these draw on the days and when I return it is always messed with. Now I used to keep some jelly packets in the front part and other condiments in a separate section of the draw. At this time the Jelly started getting smeared all over the papers in the back part of the draw. The draw is separated by a divider. So Why does this need to be bother with? Its beyond me. I brought this to my sergeants attention and as usual nothing happened.

In May, as I was trying to pass an officer on the desk, and as I was trying to walk around this officer (Sab) he attempted to kick me while he was sitting at the desk. I advised him that was not a smart thing to do regardless of the fact that he was a police officer or not. He was always in trouble for one thing or another. He was placed at the desk for light duty because of his problems and situations for discipline, yet he still carried his gun and badge.

I would be totally scared to have this kind of person with a gun and a badge next to me or facing me with one. These types of people are what protect you. Can you imagine that, what is to protect you is what you really need to fear!

On June 18, Lt. Darrel requested to know where I was when on an approved day off. I was put in the sick log when I took a Birthday Holiday off. This type of leave does not get logged in the sick log. They just wanted to make me use the sick leave so if at any time I needed it would not be there.

On July 3rd , I was advised that I am not to accept any guns for registration from the public. I am not to do inventories in the morning. I am not to handle property, or give out and accept property or equipment from the officers. I am not to handle the radio or write reports indirectly from the computer. My job on the desk is to get the property from the officers and for the officers. To do inventory and type an incident log, which is done on each shift on a daily basis.

Each shift is responsible for there own logs and inventories. I was supposed to also assist with writing reports, either from the computer or the phones or walk-ins. I had a man come into the station with a rifle and wanted to turn in the riffle. It had two serial numbers on it. This is not a usual thing, a Big-Flag went off in my head. I ran both numbers in the system and found a hit, this hit showed that the riffle was stolen. After alerting the officer on the desk that we were in possession of a stolen riffle, I gave him the information on the riffle and the information on the person. He was to handle the information from there, for I knew when I was to turn things over. I asked the person who was in possession of the riffle.

He said "It was a person in the car with him and he was a parolee and that he did not want to come into the station because if he did he knew that he would be under arrest." I wrote up the report for the gun and took it in as a recovery, Officer Arter took care of the parolee due to him being in possession of the firearm.

As this violated his probation. Part of the riffle was stolen from Kansas and part from Florida and put together here in Florida. Arter told me that was a good catch to find two serial numbers on a riffle, not many of these are found and when you find them it's a good job. If I would have been an officer I would have received an commendation for this but because of the problems they were giving me that they felt this was not warranted from then as they think they should of found it and then they would get the commendation. How greedy!!!!!!!!!!!!!!

I had no problem with things like that I can certainly work with others well, at the restaurant but not with these type of people for when they are continually cutting me down, and telling me that I am not allowed to do this or that or I'm doing the wrong thing. I would assist Officer Arter when there was a female that would come in and needed a report written, and that he might need to have a female in the room with him for their as well as his protection. I respected him highly.

Lt. Darrel questioned me on July 1st why I was answering the radio. She did not want me answering the police dispatch radio, all of a sudden. There was no reason for her to treat me this way. The dispatcher was raising us on the air for a long period of time. When there was nobody answering the radio, then Lt. Darrel finally raised the dispatcher and asked her if the response time was long before someone answered her, and was it a female who answered her request. The dispatcher replied "That she was about to send a unit to the station to see if every one was okay, because she knew that either a male officer or a female always either on the first or second call answered." When I finally answered, she asked if everything was okay, and I answered "Yes" I wanted to reply just that the Lt. Darrel did not want to allow me all of a sudden to answer you raising us on the air. I did not get the chance but wish I could of said this so I would have it recorded for internal review.

On July 15, Lt. Darrel was going through the incident logs and found an incident that had an incorrect spelled word. Upon telling me to retype it, she advised the spelling of a word, (inadvertently) and asked why I was getting the dictionary? I did not feel the word was spelled correctly, so I wanted to double check the spelling. She spell the word, while I was typing it, it still did not look correct so I checked the dictionary and her spelling was incorrect, she did not like that at all. Was I supposed to leave it spelled incorrectly? Why Should I, then have it sent upstairs spelled wrong, only to have it come back down and be asked why it is still spelled incorrectly? They would have asked, Is not Webster available?

Now it is July 16, and I went upstairs to get film to do the I D Cards for the Tow Truck Drivers. Lt. Darrel would not listen to the officer on the desk who advised her I went to go get the film. Lt. Darrel paged me to the front desk. Upon responding to the desk, she asked what I was doing. I advised her that I went upstairs to get film from the Capt's.

Office. With the film in my hand, she still was not satisfied. The Capt asked me what the problem was when he walked me upstairs to get the film, as he wanted to know what the hold up was for the completion of the Tow Truck Driver I.D. cards. When I told him I did not have any film and I went up stairs to get some and she was calling me he said "What was her problem?" I said "just another way to be on my back. She just will not let go."

On July 31st Lt. Darrel called Brathway and me in to her office to advise me that Officer Nelsaon, said "I was putting to great of expectations on her and the desk personnel, so I was not to answer the phones or ask officer on the desk to help me." I had an SCIC/NCIC class to teach and I had to keep coming out of class to fingerprint people in the lobby because the officer did not know how to run background checks on them. This was the classes I was teaching, and this officer had not gone to it yet.

However this is the classes they were suppose to have been passing and have certificates from. "If this is putting to great of expectations on these officers and that isn't it a little scary that they are wearing a gun and a badge?" You would think that they should be able to do more than you as because you are a civilian. They should be trained to do more than you are. Yet they either cannot handle what you can or do not want to handle what you can, either way the expectation should be that they are trained to do much more than you and remember they are wearing the guns and badges your not!!!!!!!!!!!!!!!!!!!!!!!!!!!!!!!!!!!!!!!!!!!!!!! !!!!!!!!!!!!!!!!

Why are they receiving certificates, just so that they can say that they went to a class? So they can say that they sat in a classroom or that maybe some of them actually will use this information and that is wonderful. But when they start using it against you and turning against you like this what do you do? Where do you go? Who helps you? Then they act like your friend! I just want to help you! HOW CAN I TRUST YOU?

# CHAPTER 13

I ASKED THAT ANOTHER civilian be put on the desk so I could teach and it was denied by Lt. Darrel. On July 19, Lt. Darrel told me that she would make a hand receipt for an individual at the window because I was currently out of receipts from the official receipt books. I went upstairs to obtain a receipt book without success. The manner in which she spoke to me was not called for and was witnessed by Lt. Carris. They must be signed out and accounted for. It would have only taken a couple of seconds to obtain a new receipt book. This person just has it in for me and will not let up.

On July 21, at approximately 10:30am I was in training a class, at the station in the training room, when Lt. Darrel walked by the room, where the class was being instructed. The officer on the desk knew I was teaching a class and would come get me when I was needed. Lt. Darrel walked by the room which has a glass window in it that you can see both ways. She saw me teaching the class and had the officer on the desk page me to the desk to ask where I was and what I was doing? Because she would not allow any one to work the desk that day, I had to keep coming out of the class and assist off Arter when he was overwhelmed. Then go back into the class.

I told the class that it would be an open book test because of the situation and that would fair be fair to them because I had to keep leaving the class. They said "It was only fair to you as well." The officer on the desk said "this is not right, that there should be someone else in here to work the desk so that you can teach the class, because the class suffers and no one else would have to teach a class like this. This is just harassment to you." I said "I know that but what am I suppose to do? She will not call any one in."

On Sept. 20th , the Station front desk called my house while I was at the doctor's office to ask for my social security number, to check up on me for being out sick. They could have either obtained this information from the payroll sheets or it could have waited for the next day for me to fill out a leave slip. This was not necessary. They did not believe that I was as sick as I was. They said that "I was faking my illness." Well this is about to get worse.

I am in the process of buying my third house now. I just sold my town house and upon signing the documents at the closing the new owners wanted immediate occupancy of the home. OH my goodness where am I going to go? I put all my things in storage and I did not know where to go. My girlfriend's mom told me to come and stay with her. Bob had a house that he had just gotten from his divorce with his wife, but I could not stay with him and I had no where to go yet he wanted me to see him and that was okay. He came home from work one day and his wife that he left me for, the one that everybody warned him about, was having an affair with someone else and he told her to pack her things and leave. He caught her in bed with this guy and then after she left the house the next day he filed for divorce and it was granted. We got back together and when his father died well that was a horse of a different color.

I have never been this sick and I really didn't know what is going on. I have never had cramps in my life. This makes no sense. I am going to the doctors and they can not figure it out either. Trust me this is not ordinary cramps. Well I am doubled over in bed, and this is not me. I am used to working two or three jobs at in one day. I cut the grass myself. I do the yard work. I have Rheumatoid Arthritis, and have had it since I was 16 but now it is real bad. This is extremely hard for me. I am at work at my Part time job, and I am bleeding by the time I get home I am dropping clots, large ones.

I called the doctor, and then took a shower. Fell a sleep with my feet in the air and the phone on my stomach. Woke up the next morning and went to his office. I had to call in sick at work. Of course I was lying and needed a doctors note. NO PROBLEM!!!!!!!!!!!!!! I got one and they did not like that. Let me tell you if you have never experienced this type of pain, you feel like someone has literally reached up inside of you and pulled everything you have right out of you, without any kind of anesthesia. You can not stand this type of pain, I don't care who you think you are.

I had a friend who had a female doctor (GYN) and she sent me to her. I said to the doctor that I mean no disrespect and I'm really sorry but I am really not comfortable with female doctors for this filed (GYN). I told her "If you don't think that you can help me then please don't touch me because it hurts so bad, that I don't want to be touched, and I just want to throw up. If you can not help me then I will go down to Jackson Memorial and sit there and wait." She said "I will do one better than that for you. I know of someone who probably can help you."

I went down to Jackson Memorial (School of Medicine) Sylvester Cancer Center. The doctor there (Dr. Tape) advised me that from his exams that I had to have an emergency hysterectomy. When I told my Sgt. at the department and put the necessary paperwork in for the leave, (you had to use all your sick leave and all your time saved that you had on the books) before you could apply for the program called the earn leave pool.

I applied for this paperwork before going to have this surgery and it was of course denied. The day before my surgery I was suppose to come to work and this application was to have been completed. It usually took me a 45 min drive to work every day, by the time I got to work I could not walk from the back door to the front desk. I was doubled over in pain and they were about to call fire rescue. I said "No, this is why I am going in the hospital tomorrow." You thought I was lying, well I suppose seeing is believing. My Sgt. just happened to be walking by and saw me trying to get to the desk. Two of my friends were near me and literally picked me up and put me on the desk. When I could walk and did not think I would have another pain like that again or worse drop another clot, they sent me home. The next day I had a total hysterectomy. I was out for three months.

I had to go to the headquarters building and talk to the department heads to see if I could get the earn leave pool because it was denied. Their response was positive I suppose after I brought them all the packages of just what I had and what I went through. My condition was diagnosed as Endometriosis. This was extremely severe and through out my entire lower abdomen area.

Upon the receipt of the package, I asked them if they had to go through this would they be able to walk or drive, when there doctors tell them not to. I was told if my brother in law called I would have gotten my earn leave pool with no problem. I told them that my brother in law does not fight my battles. They asked "who my brother in law was?" I said "for those of you who don't know he is your PBA president. But like I said he does not fight by battles. I had to have this surgery and as you can see my doctor thought it was necessary to save my life and I was told that I had to use all my time. I gave time into this program.

Now you all want to tell me that I am not worthy of getting the time when I need it. I put many years into this program and feel that I should be able to receive back from it, what I need when I need it. Now as I am in the position to really need it, I am having a difficult time getting it from you. You ask us to do walk-a-thons with you and blood drives with you numerous types of other things, when we first started in the department and everybody then wants to join on the band wagon, to be the new kid on the block. But when you really need the help this is the results you get. Boy thanks a million!!!!!!!!!!!!!!!!!!!!!!!!!!!!!!!!!!

You let all the others in the department use it when they applied for it two or three times and but when I needed it <u>just once</u> your going to deny me, how can that be? Then they asked me to leave the room while they made a decision. Yet not one of them got up to help me with the door. They said "Wait out side and we will let you know." I said "being that you are not gentleman enough to open the door, and as I have just had my insides taken out of me, as heavy as this door is it is going to take me a while to get it the door open." As soon as I can get it open I will sit out in the waiting area of your office ands wait for your decision.

Then one of them got up and came over to open the door. He apologized for not opening the door sooner and for the rest of the guys and said "Don't worry everything will be okay."

I waited outside and then they called me back in and said "it was approved and I could have it retroactive to the time of my surgery." I felt like saying how mighty nice of you, but I knew that would cause more problems, so I kept my mouth shut. (Believe me that was extremely hard to do). Sometimes you have to bite the bullet even thou they are totally wrong. I didn't feel that it was because of my brother in law that I should have gotten something that I worked so hard for and earned, that based on this information they decided that I should have received the sick leave.

When I brought the decision down to my payroll section and my supervisors in my District, Their response was "All you had to do was have your Brother in Law call for you." I said "My Brother in Law doesn't need to nor does he fight my battles in life. He's my only Brother in Law. I fight my own." I was trying to get out of the office and the door was to heavy, Remember, I just had my insides taken out and I was walking around with a pillow there to be able to stand up straight and walk as it was. I finally got a check in order to pay my bills which suffered severely because of this situation.

At this time I was working a part time job as a waitress at an Italian restaurant called Antons. I had several call customers. For those of you who do not know what a call customer is it is someone who requests your section. They are usually very sweet people. One family said to me Lee - Ann "My daughter will not eat. I do not know what to do with her. We have tried everything. We are taking her to the clinics to see if they can help her." I said "If I am not overstepping my bounds, she knows me and likes me, may I speak with her without any one being around and I will tell you later what we spoke of? I need to gain her trust first. I have been in her shoes and maybe being there she will listen and understand that there are people who what to help her get better."

My friend Louis son Pep was working in the restaurant as a busboy with me and I had a customer who was a doctor. When Pep was a little boy the kids were playing in the yard and somebody hit him in the head with a swing, and ever since then he has had a knot on his forehead that gets as red as a tomato, and he gets headaches and fevers that are un believable.

He was working with me one day and this doctor saw his head and told me that he has a tumor and it needs to be removed. I told my girlfriend and gave her the name of a doctor that he gave me. Pep told me that he would not go through this if I was not there because he was afraid he would not wake up. As He had to have his head cut open from side to side, and I really do not blame him. I promised him, I would not only be there but would be the one to wake him up, if he went through with the operation. He said "it was a deal since I had to have so many surgeries on my ankle to correct the damage I did to it."

I was there when he woke up and nobody else could wake him, not the nurses or the doctors. I made him a promise and I had to keep it. As soon as he heard my voice he woke right up. They asked me how I did this and I told them "I made him a deal, that I would be the one to wake him up and I kept my promise." They could not believe it.

Remember the young girl well her family came in again to the restaurant and told me that they were so pleased with what ever I said to their daughter, this reply was highly welcomed by me. I spoke to her later and to this day she remembers this and feels that I was feeding her as she puts it. They often thank me for feeding their daughter. I just tell them that it takes someone to be in those shoes to understand it, in order to help someone in the same shoes so they can get out of it.

You have to understand what puts you there in the first place, in order to get you out. Then you have to learn how to deal with it and accept it in order to get out of that situation. That's not always easy because it sometimes could come from family, society, or a boyfriend. No matter what the cause, serious depression can become dangerous and could cause someone their life.

That's what a lot of people just don't understand. Everyone thinks it's oh so nice to look so skinny all of the time, but to be to skinny is also too dangerous. That's bulimia and anorexia, DANGER!!!!!!!!!

I'm working at Anton and Louis calls me up to let me know that my sink in the kitchen was leaking and that her boyfriend was going to take it apart and fix it. When I got home he only took the trap off the sink and left it like that the rest of the night. I asked her son "If he wanted to go for a ride to Home Depot to get a trap so I could fix the sink?" He said "He would go for the ride. Then he asked me if I knew how to fix the sink for sure?" I asked him "Do you have confidence in me, or did you just come along for the ride?"

Either way you will see. When we got back home, I was under the kitchen sink fixing it when my girlfriend called me and her son said "Mom she's in the kitchen fixing the kitchen sink." She said "I wouldn't believe it unless I didn't see it with my own two eyes. Where did you learn how to do that?" I said "MY father taught me. If her boyfriend would have left it until the morning I would have had a flood and I just replaced the kitchen floor.

It was a lot easier to do it that night than wait for the morning. I told her "I could take out the windows in the house and replace them too if my hands would let me. I worked side by side with my dad and my brother in laws in all phases of construction work."

When Lou got her own place her daughter dropped a ring down the bathroom sink and her boyfriend took the trap off the sink to get the ring. He could not put it back together. She called me at work at Antons and asked me "If I could come over after work and fix the sink. She called her mom and asked her mother what she would do, and her mom said "I would ask Lee-Ann first because your boyfriend and your brother in law don't know how to do it."

I went over after work and fixed the sink, but I could not get the trap tight enough. As my hands have severe Arthritis in them and hurt real bad. So I called my dad and I asked him "Dad if I pick you up for breakfast, could you check and see why the sink is still leaking?" He said "You don't have to buy me breakfast I will do it for any of my girls." I then said "I will then pick you up at seven in the morning and then go to breakfast".

After having the surgery on my stomach and I was feeling better Louis and the kids and I went out for a nice dinner and a movie. We just hung out and enjoyed the time we spent with each other as this is the type of things that we like to do the most. We had such a great time and I really got tired very easily because of the surgery.

When I was able to go back to work three months later. My bills pilled up and I was in severe financial trouble. I had to work day and night in order to get back on my feet. I was tired after the surgery but I had to do this, in order to prevent everything from being lost. I called my creditors and explained the situation and they said "They would work with me." My part time job owner was very good to me. He let me work as much as I could handle. He had five different restaurants and if he needed help in any of them, he would called me and say "I need a waitress here tonight, can you fill?" Because when I first was diagnosed with this, I sat down with him and explained what was happening and asked him if I could take a leave of absence and come back after I had the surgery. He was very good to me. If I could do it now I would go back and do it again, however because of my health, I can not do it.

As Bob and his Dad had a restaurant at the time, there was this girl that came in with other girls from her office. They would have lunch every day in his restaurant. Everybody warned him that she was no good and not to go out with her but he did not listen, and then one day I went up to his apartment with my girlfriend, and I was going to leave him something special after work. When I put the key in the door and opened it up, I got the shock of my life there was this girl standing in her night gown.

I looked at my girlfriend in total amazement and said "Who are you and what the hell are you doing here?" My girlfriend looked at me and could not say anything. She was just stunned. Then she said "What are you going to do?" I said "I don't know. I just want to get in the car and go. We drove to the restaurant and I asked his father if he was busy and if he could come off the cook line." He said "Not right now sweetie, but you can go back there. " I said "It's really important and I promise I won't take long." I went back and Bob looked at me and he knew something was wrong. I said "Bob, I can not believe what I just walked into. Here is the key to your home, you can put it where the sun don't shine and never call me again. As far as you are concerned I am dead. Do you understand me ? I am not dirt and do not appreciate being treated like this."

If you have to have sluts in your home, and they have to answer your door, then you need to be protected. DO NOT CALL ME!!!!! GOOD BYE!!!! I left and apologized to his father and mother if I disrupted anybody. They said "Honey we wish you would stay and let us buy you dinner. Let us talk to you. Can we help you? We love you. We don't like this other girl he is seeing." I said "I can't help you. I am very upset." They said "Please feel free to come to the restaurant anytime you like." I said "Thank you but not now." Then I left.

# CHAPTER 14

WELL I AM BACK at work at the Hamm district, Off., Arter and I are working. As usual we work very well together. We do the inventories and then we start our day off with doing the clearance checks, I would run the checks and type the letters and get the fingerprint cards ready. Then Arter would print the people and I would have the receipts ready. If a report came to us in the middle of this it was no problem. I would run the check on the person quickly and type up the card and Arter would print the person and I would write the report.

If it was a felony report I would write the report and Arter would sign it. No problem. If it was an arrest I would fill out what I could and Arter would take over after that, it just worked like bread and butter and I think that for the most part some people do not like that we got along so well and handled the desk that efficiently. If you have two people that work side by side and work that easy together what the hell is the problem?

A few months went by and now more nonsense starts up. The administrator officer was told to come down stairs and take pictures of the shoes I was wearing. I am supposed to wear a high top tennis shoe because of the damage done to my ankle. I have a note in my file from my doctor saying that I need to wear high top tennis shoes for support. This letter was taken out and now I am having pictures taken of my shoes. My Sgt. said "Lee-Ann, this is absolutely out of line. I cannot believe what I am seeing. You need to request a copy of these pictures to be given to you in order to have them in your file, and a copy of the

119

written request to take them. Also, request to see your file and check and see if your letter is in there referencing your shoes.

If it has been taken out, then look for the date of disbursement. To see if it had been removed, then the next thing you need to do is go to the EEOC this evening after work and file a complaint. I will let you go early and I will tell them you are running an errand for me. They can not deny you that if you are doing it for me."

The next day the EEOC called the Station and requested to speak with my Supervisor and by chance Frane was the one who picked up the phone. They spoke of the incident and he told them of what had been going on. He can not stand what they are doing. He also told them that he was the one that told me to go there but it could not be said that he was the party who advised me or it would be hell for him. He was in a severe head on collision shortly afterwards while on duty. He is okay and is on light duty status work.

I am working the desk and it is Officer Arter's day off, I am working with Officer Fernandez, this particular day. We worked well together like with Officer Arter, and I did. This young lady came into the station with her three kids, and said "She needed a background check done on herself for an apartment she wanted to rent." I told her I needed her driver's license as this was the picture Identification that we accepted and considered it the most valid and current form.

It had to be valid of course. When I ran her in the system, I came up with a warrant that I believe at least ten years old. She said "That can't be mine. I don't do that anymore. I used to, but I cleaned up my act." I said "I understand that you cleaned up your act however, this is in the system and it needs to be addressed. I'll tell you what. I have been doing this for 18 years, and if this is not yours, then I apologize, but this is the way to check for sure it this belongs to you." At this point this is what needs to be done.

First the officer has to place you under arrest. Second you need to call someone to come and get your kids. Then we will take your fingerprints and fax them over to the Identification Section, and call them so that they know that we are dealing with you, so that they are expecting your prints. That way when someone sees them they will check them right away. Then they will call me back or I will call them and if the prints match the warrant then we will know that they are yours.

At that point, then we have no choice but to take you to jail and you will have to take care of it. This is the best way to handle this situation. So that is what we did. When I called warrants, the guys asked me why I was bothering them with this, because they said "You know that was her." I said "I know I was making sure, so that things went smooth on this end because of the little kids involved at the station." They were here and seeing mommy taken into handcuffs. This can be pretty devastating to a child. I was trying to buy some time to get someone here to get the kids so HRS would get not involved for any reason.

When all was said and done she thanked me for handling it in this manner, then she said "if it had to be done like this, then at least there was not a big production made out of it and not done in front of her kids, and they did not suffer. At least you looked out for them and I thank you for that, you were very courteous in the way you handled the situation."

Bob called me up and told me that his father was not doing very well. He was very sick and that he fell in the bank. They took him to the doctor and they found a spot on his lung. They had to remove part of his lung as it was cancer. He recovered from this real well.

A few months went by and as I am at the desk with Officer Arter and I really did not feel good. My face is getting redder by the minute. I have a real bad headache and it felt like I could shake a horse with it.

I never leave the desk unless I forget lunch. Most of the time, the guys would bring me a salad. They knew I was always on a diet. But today, boy I just did not feel good. I don't even care about anything. I really want to go home. What I really want to do, is to go and sit at the cemetery at my mom's grave and be at peace for a while in the calm because I can't calm down, I just don't know WHY!!!

I told the officer on the desk who is my friend Officer Arter, that I really don't feel good. I asked him "If I could take my lunch break and go to the fire station because I can not stand the noise, lights, phones and I feel like I'm going to throw up." "My face is as red as it can get, and I'm as hot as I can be." He looked at me and said "I'm going to call rescue." I said "No, never mind." Then he said "Okay." He knew me better than anybody to argue with me, that if I did not feel good there is no point in keeping arguing with me. So he called Officer Harry, one of our friends, and told Off Harry to put me and our other friend Wade in the back seat and take me to the fire station and not to put the sirens on or I would know what he was doing, and he would call ahead of time and alert rescue."

When they got me there and rescue took my pressure it was 175/155 and they said I was a walking heart attack. Rescue did not want to let me go, so I called my doctor. I told him I was on my way straight to his office and the fact that he was right next to the hospital was the only reason they let me go. So I went back to the station and got my car and went home for the day. The major was advised of what happened, and I was released on a medical sick day. I am to this date on high blood pressure medications. I wonder why!!!!!!!!!!!!!

I advised my Sgt. Braytha that I was getting more than fed up with the nonsense and I suggested it stop. Lt. Darrel was transferred to Cams Way Station shortly after.

I am on the desk, and one of the officers tells me that my uniform skirt offends him because it is to short. I advised him that it is to code. If he had a problem with it that it was hemmed per the code and to check with the SOP's on the length. It was hemmed by the county tailor. It was exactly 2 inches above my knees. I am short and when I sit down just like any body else it may look like it is shorter than the length that it is suppose to be. When does this shit stop. If I have a heart attack and drop dead then the county is the cause of it.

I am at the Hamm now in the Second Monday in July of 97. I was in the elevator around noon when a general investigation detective (Benct) came into the elevator. I thought he was just going to ride it down but when the door shut, he grabbed me and kissed me on the lips. I asked him "what the hell is this all about?" I am so furious that this happened

I got off the elevator and marched right into the armory and asked the officer if I could ask him a question. I then said Dan "I need to ask you this question?" He said sure, what's the matter. I said truthfully, "do I put this air around me that says you can touch me when ever you want where ever you want when ever you want to?" He said "truthfully, NO just the opposite, you put the air that if anyone fuck's with you that you will have trouble to deal with. Why what the hell happened now?"

When I told him he said, "oh no here we go again." I said "how do you think I feel. I just wish these guys would leave me the hell alone." "If I were dating one then it would be different for him to touch me but these guys think that they can touch you when ever they want and do what ever they want. I disagree with their feelings. I just wish this nonsense would stop. I just want to work and then go home like anybody else would. Why can't they leave me alone?" I feel like I could have a heart attack, if they don't leave me alone and this shit does not stop!!!!!!

After work that day I was having car problems getting my car started. When I got it started Det Benct asked me to meet him in a parking lot at Wal-Mart off Kenle to prove I'm not chicken. I did not meet him and I am not a chicken, I don't have any desire to have an affair with anyone. I just want to do my job and be left alone. I think these people, if you want to call them that, ought to be taught a lesson. They certainly don't have any manners. They think they can do whatever they want to because they carry a gun and wear a badge and no one will ever know because you are a little guy and you can not stand up to them.

Let me tell you we all have to answer for what we do and it will catch up to them one day. That's when you have to feel sorry for them. But I will never fell sorry for they will get what they deserve.

On Aug 8, 1997 at 5:30 am, when I arrived at work I had an officer (Fernandez) approach me and ask "What is this about you and Josh Benct?" Officer Fernandez said "That the word has it that this could be done by Det Benct." It was said "That this was Det. Benct's nature by so." On August 12, 1997 at approximately 11:00 am second civilian came into the station and applied to ride as an observer. I ran a check on her as per the appropriate procedures. Off A. J. was on the desk working that day. I asked the young lady to come into the office so I could ask her a few questions and see if a possible hit in the system was hers. It was a 100% hit as well as the possible.

I asked her if she was ever arrested for petit theft if that was the charge. She advised me that she was never arrested, so I asked her if she was PTA'd? She said "She went to court and paid fines and court fees, so I then was explaining to her that what I found in the system, it was an arrest even though she never went to jail and that sometimes they allow people with a past to ride and sometimes they don't. I explained to her that I would check and I would advise her of the decision, as I do with all civilian observers.

Off A. J at this point decided I didn't know how to tell her, or he felt that I was not necessarily handling it correctly, so he said "To give her the case number and he also wanted the paperwork, that I ran as if he were going to give her the pages. I told him I could not give her that paper work. I was going to give her a clearance letter with the case number on it and advise her how to go about sealing her record.

At this point Off A. J. advised me that I am neither an officer nor an attorney and am not allowed to tell anyone how to go about obtaining what they need. I have been on the Dept for fifteen years and I think I know what I'm talking about. If I don't know the answer I will ask someone how to handle it. When Officer Stable came back from lunch, Off A .J. wanted to Advise Officer Stable about what was going on, and or what had happened and like usual, you are talked to like you don't know what you are doing.

I opened the door and I'm so upset about a lot of different things that are going on at the stations and the door opened harder than I expected it too and it sounded like I deliberately slammed the door. Officer Stable advised me that we should talk to Lt. Haner inside because it was not the place to talk about it outside. I told the Lt. and Officer Stable that I don't like being under minded by anybody. Officer

Stable has done this several times to me and I don't feel I can trust him. I don't tell him anything for just that reason.

On Aug 15, I called Paras at Internal Review (IR) to ask the status of my investigation was it over and she said she would contact me when it was over, and I could read the case. She said "That Major Donel said I was talking about the case. I told my Lt. Haner that I took the case to I R when he came back from vacation, so he could be advised. I was told that I was talking about the situation and that I should not talk about the situation to any one. It was his watch and I thought he should know. He was a very fair person and would be on your side if you were right not the others side. Everything is only the way of course they want it to be. One sided.

On 8-18-97 at 13:56 I took my personnel belongings out to my car and when I came in with clothes to change into to go to therapy from a injury while at the county, which I'm suppose to do and do the therapy on county time not mine. Capt. Lillerman asked Officer Arter what my work schedule was. He said "it was from 06:30 to 3:00 pm according to the line up. Off Arter was on Vacation, when I got injured and was not aware that the Lt. (Hanner) let me adjust my times to 5:30 am to 2 pm Mon/Wed/Fri for therapy. Captain Lillerman then asked Officer Stable my current hours as it Stg was in and he advised him that it was Sgt. Stable's day off. I left and went to therapy.

I had put in my request for training to go to instructors training workshop class as they have repeatedly put me in training positions on this department. As many times as I have put in my request for this class it has been denied. Captain Lillerman said "being that I instruct these classes I should go to one of these classes and be signed up to take the next class."

Upon my major seeing this she was not too happy with this decision and wanted to reject it until we fought it saying that my certificates would be in violation if I did not get into one of these classes. The next class that was set up I was signed up for and it was just another hassle that was not necessary to have to go through.

When I was advised, I advised by Irish. He said "He would check with Capt. Lillerman to advise him when the class was set. At these times he asked Capt Lillerman and found out that the class would be set for the week of Sept 9-97, to 9-23-97.

On 9-8-97, I received a call from Tina Scrol at the training Bureau advising me that I was scheduled for the Sept 1-26 class. At this point Capt. Lillerman advised Irish that I could not go to the class. This is the class I was advised by Capt. Lillerman in July to make sure I got into because they would not allow me to go into the July class. Capt. Lillerman then stated the fact that I go to therapy three times a week for a county related injury and it's on my time not the county time, which should be on county time.

All with out my knowledge or Officer Arter, Sgt. Irish while upstairs was hooked up to a kid web site on his computer, at his desk while at the station. All of a sudden he was then transferred down to the front desk. It was brought to the administrations attention that He continued to used this site and would of course change his screen to his screen saver when anyone of us walked by, so that we would not know that he was still doing nor alert anyone. Then all of a sudden the site comes up on the computer on the desk and as officer Arter and I not knowing about it, was surprised. Irish plugged his personal computer into the phone line on the desk and was again hooked up to the web site.

Now after all the investigations were completed and done, the total outcome was that he could retire on a medical and keep his pension without going to jail or serving any time. So I guess you can say that the system is only for the ones that they invest in wouldn't you say? I feel sorry for his wife and daughter. Now you know anyone else would have had a full blown trial it would of been on the news and then found guilty and would be serving some hard time. But not this one.

Now as you have another officer who worked the desk at the Hamm district who continually gets himself into trouble and yet he still has his gun and badge and as he should not have them. Now, He was placed on the desk because he could not stay away from his wife's new boy friend and his kid's at the ball field. I understand that these are his kids, but he needs to separate the fact that these are hers as well.

She has decided to move on and he needs to as well. He met someone else and when he finally did, he got the new persons phone number and then this person decided she did not want to see him any more. When she changed her number, all of a sudden he came up with the new unpublished number.

This caused a problem, and he was placed on the desk again. At this time, I advised the officer at the desk, his name is Off Goodinthall that maybe he should speak to the Sgt and have his I.D. number blocked, in the system so that he could not run subject checks any more as this would help with the problems and stop them form arising.

They both agreed with me and this was done with the administrations authority. He was pushing his police authority to get what he wanted, saying that it was part of an investigation and that it was needed. He did this so he could obtain all the information, and you think that these people who thought they were protected were as they thought. (NOT)

When the party was paying for a non-published number, the supervisor at the phone company was not supposed to give out this number. If the supervisor would have found out what the situation was related to and why there was a police officer asking for the number? Then the phone number would not have been obtainable by this officer and the number would have remained unpublished, but he would then have one of his detective friends do this so for him so as not to get his-self in more hot water. These little things went on and on and yet nothing was done too drastically about it.

I would get requests from the First Lt. to run information in the computer, like asking me "If I could run information on his son's drivers license to see if it was valid or not." This is not necessarily allowed. However this is my first Lt. I would get requests from other officers asking me to run information on someone they would want to meet. This is also not permitted, however I am a non sworn personal and they are sworn so I do as I am asked.

Well, it so happened that this Officer who was placed on the desk because he was in the process of getting the divorce. As He had kids with her, all of a sudden he was at the ball games, he was not supposed to be near them. Now this caused a big problem. Even more so because he ran the new boyfriend in the system and saw something he should have not seen.

When he brought this information up in court the ex wife was livid, as I'm sure anyone would be and wanted to know where and how he obtained this information. She came to the station and asked the Sgt "if he was able to obtain this information in the system on his own, and if he was just allowed to go into any ones files at any time he wanted to?" This again put him back into Internal Review and again on the desk.

If I found any warrants on any subjects I would always give them to the proper agency and have them pick up the subjects. I think that they made up a false warrant in the system to try and trap me, so that I would continue to run the warrant and see how many times I would run it, even thought I would send the information to warrants bureau and to the Police Department but they did not know that I would send it to the Dept as well. I do not believe that they would think that I was that close with any of the officers at any other departments, so I could send the information to them. When they found out that I did send them there the scam back fired in there face.

This is the kind of person that is carrying a gun and badge that is protecting and serving you as a police officer. Are you really safe? Can you really sleep at night? I would feel safer in the grave yard. At least they are not going to come and get you. He was not stable enough to stay away, he has a restraining order from a judge against himself, and so what do you think that if he had to enforce them on some one else do you think he did enforce them or if he felt that the other person could help him that he just let it slip by?

While Off Goodinthall was on the desk, we had a prisoner come into the station. He was arrested for a traffic infraction. This was not unusual. It really was not a big deal, but this person must have had other issues that he could not handled being in a cell, and somehow he placed his shirt around his neck and hung himself. Upon checking the prisoners, we discovered this and of course an investigation was done and Off Goodinthall was cleared. He did nothing wrong. The prisoner kept saying "Please get me out of here, I can't take this" and we kept saying "You would be transferred soon" but we never thought that he would have hung himself. This was very tragic for the entire precinct felt bad maybe because some were guilty of other things and this shook them up for once, and they saw that things could get to a person.

On August 15, I called Sgt. Paris again at Internal Review to ask the status of my investigation was it over with Detective Benct. She said "She would contact me when it was over and I could read the case." My Lt was the only administration person I trusted. It is funny that officers keep coming to me and tell me that they keep hearing this and that about the case and that the Detective is known to do these type of things, however if I were to say something to the LT. I am talking about the case.

WHERE IS THE JUSTICE IN THE SYSTEM OF THE ADMINISTRATION?????????

Nothing was said about the situation with Officer Benct after that and he never bothered me again, however he was back in the station in the detective bureau, amazing isn't it. Trust me it doesn't matter how much you know, or how you acquired your knowledge, whether it was from watching and learning or going to classes or schools, if you just picked it up by trial and error.

It really didn't matter, knowledge is knowledge and if your not part of the click you are just shit out of luck no matter what you do or say. Remember they did not want to tel my wrights nor did they tell me, that I was allowed to file a complaint or that it was available for me as a victim, they never would take it to that level only saying it but not accepting that I was a victim of sexual harassment because they did not want that out in the news. That one of there officers was being brought up on sexual harassment. That the harassment was going on for TEN years, and that he did not know when to STOP. That he should have known better.

# CHAPTER 15

YET HERE I GO again I am in need of a part time job again, so I asked a friend if she knew someone who was looking for a secretary. She said that she would look around. Well after meeting the party who was "SUPPOSE" to be an attorney, if he had any extra typing or filing that I could do or if he knew of any body, she said he would let me know?

I was interviewed by this supposedly attorney and He said "okay No problem you are very smart and have the skills I need so when can you start". Now he wanted me to help at the Spanish festival and go to Cyaocho and help distribute papers, for his broker lending business. This was an all day affair and I told him "that I could not do that because I can not stand the heat. From the sun all day. I do not bake in the Fla. heat." "That I would collate papers together for him for this occasion till all hours of the night as this was Friday night and I could stay late."

So he would have it ready for Saturday and Sunday. He never gave me any money for this. I was to do some typing for him and I did but I never got one red cent form this man. Now his secretary and her husband and I were there until all hours of the night collating these papers. He was showing us how to print on T-shirts while we were doing the papers. There were a lot of papers upstairs and for some reason he would not let us go upstairs.

So all I did was put papers together. He asked again "if I would be there tomorrow" and I said again "No I told you I can not stand to be in the sun all day." I will be at home. This man never paid me for any of the work I did including for collating these papers.

He asked me "if I could check the contents of the paper work that needed to be filed to the state, and make sure that it was correct when someone came into have their record expunged?" I said "all I would be able to do is to make sure that the fingerprint card is typed out correctly." "I can make sure that the charges are correctly filed in on the form and that it is for the correct person." That I could not guarantee if the matter would be sealed." I could only make sure that the paper work is does right and there could not be any grantee that what you are seeking to be done would be sealed ."

That is all I can do. There is no harm in this, I thought. Who would of known!!!!!!!!! I found out that while we were collating the papers there were two men asking questions about me up stairs in his office on 8th Street in the Ocean Bank where he did his business and also ran the office with an other attorney Blade and Lewhitch, and I wondered what it was all about.

# PART C

NOW IF YOU THINK THAT WHAT YOU HAVE ALREADY READ IS NOT A FORM OF CORRUPTION THEN YOU MUST REALLY READ THE REST TO GET A BIRDS EYE VIEW OF JUST HOW CORRUPT THINGS ACTUALLY ARE !!!!!!!!!!

Now as I met this supposed attorney, he told me he was an attorney from New York. We met for coffee, I did not know that he was not allowed to drive. I did not know he was a habitual traffic offender and did not have a driver's license. Since I did not see his car and as he had someone drive him to the restaurant, he told me that his car was broken down.

The second lie that he told me. I did not know this was not true so I accepted his story that his car was broken down and that he was telling me the truth. His secretary was with us when we collated the papers, so I really didn't think anything of this situation. This bastard yes forgive me for my language but he is just that a real bastard and so are his to lying friends they were just setting me up for something that I had no idea of.

His secretary told me not to come to his office because two guys were coming by and asking a lot of questions about my being there. They said "Questions like what was I doing and what was I being paid to do? They said "she is not getting paid to do anything. He does not pay her. She just checks the paperwork before it is submitted." What was wrong with that? I was just trying to pay my bills.!!!!!!!!!!!!!!!!!

I would run subject checks in the system and I would find warrants in the system. I would do the research on the paper work and if they had a warrant send them to the police station. If the warrants had any other information on it that might be good, I would hold on to it and send it to the proper department that handles this. I did this anonymously with the last known updated information on the subject. Then I would give it to the proper person. If it was someone in the district, I would give it to the officers in the district, they would do the right thing with the warrant. If it was a traffic warrant they would take care of it.

If it was a felony warrant they would take care of it as well. I always took care of warrants that I found in the system. If someone came into the station, and they had a warrant, I would turn it over to the officer on the desk. If I were left alone on the desk, I would get an officer to handle the situation from somewhere, somehow either from the administration section, or the school resource office, or I would call one in off the road.

If it were in an other entity, I would contact that entity and have someone come by and obtain the information, that way they could take care of the warrant as this is not allowed to be sent in the mail.

# CHAPTER 16

WELL, I HEARD THAT the Attorney that I was trying to do some typing for had a Felony past. Now If this is true, I was not allowed to work for him, so I asked someone who worked with him. But they did not know the truth either so to no prevails. Now the two other parties would not tell me the truth Bark and Blade kept this to them self and had no intention of telling me that this person was or was not a felon. I tried to protect myself. Let me tell you these guys are vicious, Very vicious.

So I ran his name to see if he was a Felon. Now Remember how many times the officers would come to me to run someone for them whether it was a current situation or in the past or if it was family, or to run someone so that they could meet someone.

Well what was the harm in me checking to see if this individual was a felon or not? I would of stopped associating with him right away and let the secretary know what was going on. Is it not what is good for the goose is good for the gander? I forgot or excuse me I forgot that it's the police department, and if you don't get along with them you are screwed. Bob, I really have to thank you for standing by me throughout this.

What about the officer that ran his ex-wife's new boyfriend, found out that he had a past, did not like the fact that he did, this causing him some trouble on the ball field. What about the fact that when he met someone new he found out this new persons phone number after she had it changed by the phone company because she did not want to see him any more? Pulling police strings is against the rules however this goes on all the time. So when I tried to find the truth what do you think happened to me. Read on and you will see the corruption and just to what limit they take an outsider too.

Well there was an officer that worked for the City of Sunlakes just recently that ran 121 suspects at the States Attorney's office, and was not arrested or lost any pension. Nothing happened to him from the state attorneys office which is under Katherine Rundle, she just made an inquiry about it. There were no charges against him for any illegal usage of the computer, he wasn't fired for it either.

He was not forced to lose his pension for this. He was not put in jail or on trail for this. He did not lose his gun or badge. He wasn't placed on a desk job permanently. He wasn't reduced to a lower status or asked to resign and leave the department.

WHERE IS THE JUSTICE??????????????????

Believe me when I tell you that there are double standards for sworn personal and non-sworn personal. They treat non-sworn personal like garbage. If you are in there loop or the click and they like you, there will be no problem. If for some reason they don't like you well there will be a world of hell to pay. There really is no other way to put it. It is these people that are protecting you. They protect and serve you, are you being protected and served? If so HOW?

I understand that there are some good cops but where do you draw the line? Where does the nonsense stop? When should this nonsense have been stopped? Should all this crap have been going on? Was this all necessary? Is this what you have to put up with in order to have a pension and retirement? If I came to work and did my job, and they did, and they did not like me for whatever reason, what was I suppose to do? Just leave my job because they did not like me? Are you supposed to throw in the towel because of this?

Well you soon will know just how corrupt Blade and Lebwitch truly are and what really goes one. Bob called me today and he is very upset and I asked him "honey what is wrong?" He said "let's meet for dinner I have to talk to you. I met him for dinner and he told me that his father is dying of cancer and that he and his mom did not want anyone at the house and he would be staying at there house until his father passed."

He said "that his father was extremely ill and that His mom did not want any one to see his dad in this state of his life." I said "I truly understand and told him to extend my feelings to his mom and offer my assistance in any manner that I could be to the family." I understood because of what had happened with my mother and Bob knew that. He told me that he would extend this to his mom and he appreciated it deeply. He would call later and I could call the house and talk to him later if I wanted but not past a certain hour of the night. He would call me if it were later than 9:00pm as not to upset his father. I told him I perfectly understand.

Throughout all of this, I have always been called one of "Jerry's Kids" in a sarcastic way Meaning Jerry Lewis Kids because I have always had to wear braces of one sort or another. I have had to have them on because of my Arthritis which has never slowed me down to where I have not worked. Nor did I stop working until the year of 2000 when I went into those episodes of Congestive Heart Failure five times in one year.

There is no history of CHF in my family. The only explanation is because of the stress. I have nothing against Jerry Lewis' kids. I think it's a wonderful thing what he does for the kids. Just because he takes the time to care, maybe they should go to a round church where the devil can't corner them. For I'm afraid there prayers would never be answered. I'm sorry they don't have to answer to me, they have to answer to the man that put them on this earth and I sincerely hope they can.

I am outside of the Attorney's office with my sister and this person Kevin who said "Hey I just got a new truck, would you like to see it?" We all said "Sure, let's go after being in the office where she worked said hay come outside and see my new car." It was a Cadillac Escalade. What a beautiful vehicle. Kevin then took money out of his pocket, as if he was going to hand it to me and my sister said "Wahoo take this inside and count it and I will make a receipt for it." You are not going to count money in this parking lot, so that I will be robed or killed by the neighbors as they know I work real late here and am alone most of the time.

So Kevin took the money inside, it was given to Bark the man who told me and my sister he was an attorney and my sister made the receipt, Not me. I never touched the money. I did not count the money. I only looked at the car. I told him it was nice, and to use it in good health.

My sister later testified to the fact that Bark was the one who took possession of the money and she makes the receipt for the money. She testified I never took or received the money. Kevin set me up and said that I took it while I was looking at the truck, and went back inside to the office and then went home. Here's is where it gets juicy, the next morning at the station Kevin came to me and asked me to sign a fingerprint card for him, as he came to me as if he was my boyfriend.

He had taken the fingerprints of someone and he did not want to come into the station because he was known as snitch. Some of the other officers and I did not know that he was a snitch nor what was going on. If I had known this then I would have been alerted to their (The PD's) little operation and it would have been broken up. As I would not meet him in a parking lot down the street he thought it was better to do this in front of the station.

Two days later the two guys that were asking questions before at the office on 8th Street where I was to work for the attorney Bark, came into the station and went into the Captain's office and said "we need to speak to Lee-Ann, so they called me up and I went off the desk and into the Captions office." They said "You know that I am Detective Joe Smith, and Detective Juan Jones from Internal Review."

"We have a Warrant for your arrest." I said "What a what, what are you talking about? I did not do anything? What is going on?" They said "You have been around with Mr. Bark and he is a felon and since you are working with him that is cause for a warrant for your arrest.)

We received this tip that you were hanging around a felon and we checked it out, and since we discovered this we had to have a warrant for your arrest. Do you remember running his name in the computer? Yes or No? "Did You know that this is against the rules and regulations." I said "and how many times have others done the same, and how many of the different officers on the department illegally use the computer for there personal use and they are not arrested? I was only trying to protect myself and see if this individual was a felon, because I was told this might be true and after running his name I found out it was true and had no intent to hang out with him or help him again."

This did not matter to them as they wanted me off the department anyway. If they don't like you, you don't have a chance in hell to protect yourself no matter how hard you try. Remember that my brother in law once told me that when he made PBA president my troubles would be worse when certain people found out that I was connected to him, because they did not like him, but I did not care about them. They can all learn that they have to stand up for there own actions that they cause. Their comments were that they finally got me as they were walking me out the door.

NOW HERE IS WHERE THE DOUBLE
STANDARD REALLY SETS IN.

They took me to the jail and when they had me in the cell the jailers said to me, "What are you doing here?" They knew me because of the bond hearing paperwork that I had done for many years. They said "you do not belong in this situation." They would leave the door open and tell me to go and get water as often as I needed it. They would tell me to go and use the phone several times.

When it came time to talk to the nurse and she found out exactly what type of medicines I was on, she said "get this lady out of here you do not want her in here, and have this on your hands." She further said "She is extremely sick and should not be in here. What is she here for?" When they found out they could not believe that they arrested me because I ran someone in the system to see if the person was a felon, and tried to protect myself.

Kevin said "I took a Bribe from him because he did not want to pay to have his case expunged." As I suspected and it turned out when you are a snitch your really are just a "bastard."

Remember I was at work and they took me straight to jail. They make you tear apart your shoes and make sure that you are not carrying any weapons. They tear apart your bar and make sure that there are no weapons in your bar. They will strip search you to make sure that you are not carrying any drugs in or on the body and make you bend over and cough so as to make sure that you did not put drugs up your bottom and carry them in that way. This was exceptionally humiliating and if you did not do this it would get worse for they don't care.

After making the one call they are suppose to give you I was able to reach my sister and she helped to set the bond in motion. She also paid the fee and put her house up for security as this was required for the type of charges I was charged with.

The nurse wrote on the card that I was bonding out and needed to be released immediately. She said "do not transport as this woman she is too sick, If transporting she will wind up in JMH."

When my sister told Bark and Blade what happened they said oh do you have the money to help her or do we have to help and you can work off the fee. I do not know exactly how she got the money and how she got the bails bond men to help so fast but she did.

I did not want to go to the hospital ward of the jail as this was not necessary. I was being bonded out and could not wait to get out of there. When the bail bonds man came and got me, I hung on to him for dear life and asked him not to let me go as my knees were getting weaker and weaker by the minute. I thought that I was going to have a heart attack. I was so scared. I asked him to just drive and get me out of this county and I never wanted to look back as far as I was concerned.

Needless to say I am not with this department any more. I have no desire to see any of these people any more. This chapter in my life is a closed book now as I must move on and go forward.

They arrested me for running this individual for checking to see if he was a felon and trying to protect myself. Remember that I had sexual harassment charges against two different officers, and they don't like this and if you don't get along with them you are not following the rules.

Bark was arrested for felony DUI and sent to federal prison. But there is more to this, while I was being tried the original attorney that I went to see, to try to finds this part time job is a worse bastard than

Bark. Can you imagine that!!!! He forced his secretary my sister to lie to me and tell me that Bark was in the hospital with a heart attack, and that no one was allowed to see him. And unbeknown to my sister he made this ball faced lie to her. She was to tell the same to all the clients.

As things started to really unravel the truth came out in court. But things like this also caused him to have to shut down his business for two months as the judge in his trail said he is like a "Petri dish" that he sets up his clients all the time. So why not do it to me?

Who I thought I was, just his secretary's sister so what, you think that he did not try to harm her as well, thinks again. For this attorney thinks only of himself and how he can keeps the client coming to him for the need for more legal work. He dose not care about the kind or the amount of damage he does to anyone, for the more he can control the situation and create havoc the better he likes it.

He thrives on and gets off on causing trouble, he is so lazy, yes I said lazy that he pushes all of his work of on others just because he wants to be able to blame someone else for the situation.

The police department is no different for they will do anything to get you out. Eventually I was allowed to seal this after all was said and done as though nothing happened but it still sticks in my mind. How can you erase what they did to you when you see even one of them? It is just a constant reminder of all of it. I will go on you can bet on that I will not be around any of them, I will never have to see them again. Funny how these people get away with all of this and nothing happens to them. It will come back to haunt them though, I can promise you that.

# CHAPTER 17

OH YEA, LET ME tell you about the attorney Blade who was suspended for two months and then on probation for two years, not for what he did to me but for what he did to others. And as of the writing of this book he is up for an 18 month year suspension for allowing his cohort in another case to perpetrate a crime against a doctor for extortion. Yes I said "extortion". He allowed his cohort to write this extortion letter and did not do anything to prevent this disbarred attorney from doing this.

He also tried to have me commit a crime against the bankruptcy court. Because he was too lazy to do the proper job and did not want to correct his previous error. So my sister and I went to the court and corrected it by ourselves. When we complained to the State Bar about him they did nothing saying his response was valid and so it stayed in his folder and when the extortion came up they used this against his as well. As well two other people who filed complaints of how he sets people up in order to get them to come in for more legal work, of course they do not know it is due to his mistakes that they need him again.

Maybe some times you can see the reward of justice but it can take along time to see and then you can not be sure if it is your reward or someone else's.

I had a four bedroom home and I sold it to be with Bob. We were going to get married and adopt a child as I can not have any nor can he now. Until we get married I would be living in an apartment, as I needed a roommate, this friend who was suppose to be a good and trust worthy friend that, oh yea he really showed his true colors for he became the roommate from hell. He said "he was going to pay half the rent and utilities" and that would have been great if he really did just that.

I had a second hand truck and it was getting to small and run down and as I have to have a car to get around in Bob wanted me to have his. I told my roommate I would sell him mine and he could owe me the money, he could transfer the vehicle into his name as he had a son and needed a decent car to get around with. Well he did not like the fact that as I was coming home from work one day, and I had not had the chance to change the tag on the car yet and as I was headed to the go to the tag agency and I got into an accident, which stopped me from getting there.

I was literally across the street from where I was to be when the accident occurred. He caused so many problems because of the accident that I had to place a restraining order on him and have him removed from the apartment.

The night the restraining order was served he put his son through the window and the neighbors called the police, they were thinking that someone was breaking into my apartment. I had a little dog and he would not allow me to go and get him out of the house. I was so upset and I told the Judge that he would not let me get the dog, when I finally got the dog he was bleeding from the back end. The Judge wanted to know if he hurt the dog because he was going to charge him with animal cruelty.

I had to take B. J. (the dog) to the vet and have him checked out to see if he was okay. The vet said "he was very nervous due to the situation at the home, but he was not abused." I said "thank goodness." B. J. was so funny and such a good dog, he was just like a little human. I had to give him to my sister's son to take care of him because she could not have pets in her condo. As the situation was I had to leave the apartment and she told me I could move in with her that way I would be helping her and she would be helping me.

Well I lived with her for eighteen months and then all of a sudden we met this young lady who needs a place to stay for two weeks, so we said she could stay at the house and the young lady then with out permission brought in her boyfriend. I was told that they were going to pay her a little more money than I was, so my sister wrote me a letter and told me that I was to leave her house because the baby powder and the air condition was truly out of control. I swept the baby powder up the minute I put it on in the bathroom so it was not on the floor.

When I was there she had to have her bathroom remodeled. I really don't care how she spent her money, but if someone else is going to pay you more than I, don't blame it on powder and the air conditioner. She did not even have the nerve to tell me this. This was typed and taped to the TV in my room as she would not even speak to me. Then this young lady, we will call her Marta, Marta told me to giver her key to the house back. I told her that I would give the keys to the house to my sister as she gave them to me and she will deal with me not to any one else.

Marta kept calling me at work to ask me what time was I getting off, to ask when was I getting my furniture out of the house so she could have a dinner party at my sister's home with her mom and her boyfriend. This is how I was treated after I went to stay at my sister's house, after having being thrown out of an apartment that I rented for myself eighteen months prior. Unbeknown to me Marta had stole form my sister, and had told my sister that I had told her that I wanted to move out.

That my intent was to share the stolen money to repay me for what I had paid her for the past eighteen months. Several days later I found out my sister threw out Martha and the boyfriend after calling the court on them and reporting the theft. Then finding out that the boyfriend was being placed on house arrest and had to be in the home all the time. My sister never gave them the key to her home. Martha was to only be there for two weeks, but in those two weeks she sure caused a lot of trouble and if it had not been for her I probably would still be living with my sister.

Well Bob and I have not gotten married yet and we meet in Georgia and South Carolina. His job still has him all over. Just when he thinks he will be settling into one town his boss has him moving into another. Now he is moving to Minnesota.

I truly miss Bob. This is getting harder and harder on both of us. Give me a ticket for an air-o-plane. I don't have time to take a fast train. Lonely days are gone. I'm a going home. My baby wrote me a letter. I don't care how much money I have to spend. I have to get back to my baby once again. Lonely days are gone I'm a going home to be with my baby.

I have another sister who owns a business and again I am working part time I worked at the same store for quite some time. I worked with quite a few kids. They never knew what happened to me. I never told them and it was not for public knowledge. I worked threw it keeping it inside as much as possible and not letting it on. I had the respect of the community and the kids that worked for me. This was and is very important to me. My girlfriend stood beside me every step of the way knowing everything that happened. All that was done to me and every little piece of garbage they did.

Now there is Louis who lived with me for years. Her kids respect me very highly and knew what happened yet they say this was not true because they knew what I went through at the department for all those years. Now all the kids that work for me here only know me from being around me here. They know that if they needed something I would give them the shirt off my back yet do not stab me in the back for I will not be there for you. I do unto others as I would have them do unto me.

Hurricane Wilma came along and I started a box of clothes. I went through all the clothes that I had and whatever I could not fit or would not wear regardless if it was brand new or not I put it in a box and all the people in the neighborhood joined in, my box was so big that my firefighter friends came and took the clothes to the drop off center because I could not lift it in the car, and it was too full to get it in the truck.

I know a young lady named Brittany and she wrote a letter to the local TV station telling them of the humanitarian actions that I have done and the situation that I am in. She was trying to see if they would assist in me any way to help get a house from the humanitarian program where you go and get assistance by putting in hours and if they can award the correct person a home they give the most needed person that home.

They responded back to her asking what happened to me but she never responded back. I lost the chance for that home and had to live in a hotel room on the highway. I can not afford my medicine as it was too expensive.

I cleaned the Dairy Queen after the hurricane because we lost power and believe me that was not fun with all that sour milk and then helped my friend open his Subway restaurant to get the neighborhood food for those who were without power. I did what I could to help anyone that I could. Everybody knew that if they needed something I would do what I could, the kids came around and asked if I needed help and told me that I did not have to pay them, that they just wanted to help me just because I will always make sure that they have something when they need it.

Like a glass of water if it is too hot outside. A little extra change if they need it for the item they maybe buying out of my tip jar. The parents would come back and give it back to me in more ways than one.

Brittany knows that I do not have a home and that I was literally on the streets with no where to go. My family did not take me in, I helped my sister after her husband died, but when I needed a place to live she would not let me stay with her. I had my four bedroom home and Louis was living with me with her kids, I made sure that I had room for my sister, yet when I was in desperate need she would not make room for me or help me. Well that's okay, because I truly believe that we all have to answer to someone higher than us on this earth and she doesn't have to answer to me.

I am struggling to make it threw and I know for sure there is always some way, I will with the help of the man above looking over me. This you can count on.

Brittany does not work with me any more and I do not know how to get in touch with her. At the time that she did, she wanted to do something special for her parents for Christmas so she asked me if I still embroidered and I said "yes." She then asked me if I would embroider two songs on a two different canvases for her parents.

I took the words to Butterfly Kisses and then put little butterflies all over the canvas for her dad. Then I took the words to I can not think of the name of the other song but the meaning of the song is, she is looking up to her mom and I put her mom on the top and her on the bottom of the canvas. She said "her parents could not believe that she had these made for them and as she could not afford to have them framed, they would pay for the framing." That meant a lot to them and me. Brittany and the girls and I all got along very well.

My other customers all think of me as their Dairy Queen Lady. They all have known me for about ten years. I have worked in this area for about twelve years. Most of the kids have known me for about that time and they call me by my first name. If I need something they are always there to help me. As I told you I have been in a few car accidents and gotten hurt. I am not allowed to lift anything heavy so they help me when I have to lift something.

The little faces are so innocent. They do not know any better and all they know is that the lady that hands them ice cream is either nice or mean to them and that is all they need to know. That is the way I kept it. When they come in I want it to be friendly and exciting. Some of the children that come in are Autistic and it needs to be fun.

They come in and get Superman Ice cream. We put a cape on and pretend that we are flying. We have a little school down the walk way and the little ones come in and we have school field trips. I joke with the kids telling them that we have a cow in the walk-in and they think that I actually have a cow in their. I show them how I make Ice cream and some of the cakes. Then I take them in the walk-in, I show them how cold it is and joke about the cold. They all start laughing and joking that it' so cold!!!!!!!!!!!!!!!!!!!!!!

Sometimes we have a bunch of little lunches depending on the ages so they won't choke on the hot dogs and if there parents sign a wavier saying they can have a hot dog lunch, they come down and have that lunch. It's pretty sad now a day's that a kid can not even have a hot dog lunch with out having to have the parents sign a wavier that they are not going to sue because they went to have a lunch on a field trip.

As I am writing this, I am facing another challenge; I possible must go through another fusion on my ankle. It is still in trouble. Believe it or not, it now has that major arthritis that the doctor told me about several years ago. It would have back in '92, it is now 2005. It is suspected that I will have to go and have another major surgery on my ankle and I hope that the Good Lord is on my side and that I will not have to lose my foot. I'm sure that the team of doctors as well as God is on my side. I will not loose my foot. I have diabetes to contend with as well. This is just a few of the problems that I must deal with every day. NO one ever promised you a bed of roses.

Remember that I was in trouble and the department forced to me resign well the reason for this was that when they arrested me, they said "That I was charged with Bribery, and illegally using the computer." Now is that a real double slap in the face or for double jeopardy or what. I almost met my maker because of this. When I sat in the living room and my other sister (I have several) said to me 'Lee-Ann doesn't sit down, what ever you do, get to the hospital now. I'm calling fire rescue." After her statement "I replied to her "NO, I'll drive myself. I don't feel good." When I got to the hospital the nurse took me in and took my pressure. It was very high and I was getting literally bigger in size by the minute.

Let me tell you this and I mean it in all sincerity. This is the kettle calling it literally black. When I got into the hospital that day the nurse looked at me and I said "excuse me I do not feel good. I feel like you could put a pin in me and I could explode in a New York minute." She took my blood pressure and when she tried to pump the cuff I thought my head was going to explode. She called the doctor and he came out and said "do not alarm her but get her back here immediately. She is about to have a heart attack."

They took me back into the ER and gave me medicine and watched me for about six hours. I had to let loose of an extreme amount of water and go through a lot of tests before they would let me go upstairs they then kept me for a week. I lost 25 pounds that week of water from around my heart alone. That's how much stress I was under from all of this.

I had another attack of Congestive Heart Failure so the doctors said "I had to have a balloon put in my heart to check and see if there was a blockage, so that they could see what was causing this, or if this was just stress related. I was being transferred from one hospital to another via Randell Eastern ambulance service with a tube in my body. They checked to see if there was a blockage which thank God there was none. The machine in one hospital broke and I had to be moved to another hospital to perform the procedure.

There was no blockage and no reason for the CHF so I was hospitalized for a week. I had no idea that I had a court date at this time and that it was set and my attorney did not know either, so the police came to the house and said I missed my court date, and arrested me again. I took my hospital papers to the judge and told him that I was undergoing a surgical procedure to see why I was going through CHF and that I was being transferred to another hospital at the time I was suppose to be in court, and that I had no idea that I had a hearing and he excused all those related charges.

That does not erase all the horror in your mind of what they put you through, for nothing because of there mis - communication. I was in the jail for three days. Do You Truly think that they really care, because they could care less. All they want is that they look like the good guys when they are wrong.

This is the Medical terminology for what I had, Cardiac Trponin. It may be increased by any condition causing myocardial cell damage, including congestive heart failure, unstable angina, remedy is see the carditis and have cardiac surgery. Believe me if you thought I wasn't scared, and that I thought I was going to die, Then you are not thinking right, for I thought that, if that is what is to be, so be it.

Remember, thou all the times they wanted me to run information for them so they could meet someone they wanted to meet. Get information on their own family members; find out information on land, what ever the case may be. I did what was asked. I was a non-sworn personal. I did not cause problems, just received a lot of them. The condition of my medical status was not good. When I came out of the hospital, I felt better. I did what I had to. I exercised like I was told to. I even cut the grass every week. Well, all of a sudden, here we go again, I'm going back into, CHF and the doctors couldn't figure it out.

While I was under arrest for the second time, I sat in a holding cell with these other ladies. In this cell you have no privacy. If you have to go to the bathroom you share the ca-mode. These ladies would all stand around you because they would not allow us to shut the door. The door had to be open at the time for processing. We had one person in particular that was causing a lot of problems and she just did not want to be there. Then they take you to another cell where they make three of you stay in a room for the night.

Two slept on the floor on a mat and one sleeps on the hard cell bed. Then they transferred us to another place where we were supposed to be housed and if you were getting out you would be let out from there. I was getting bonded out so I was not to be taken there however they transferred me there anyway. When I got there I was still in the state of Congestive Heart Failure and the ladies in the cell did not understand what was happening. My face was as red as I could possibly be. They told me that I should have lain on the floor face down because it was cold enough and they thought that I was having a heart attack.

I did not receive any of the medicine that I take and I take thirteen different medicines a day. I brought one dose of medicine with me and when I was released, I took the medicine bottle and then took my medicine. When I was outside there was an officer who asked me what was wrong. I said "I did not have any change to make a phone call." He said "Here is my cell, someone like you should not be here in this area without a phone and does not belong here anyway. Call whom ever you need to so you can get a ride and get them to get you out of here." I could not wait to get home and take a shower and wash my hair. I never want to see any of these people again. My sister came and got me.

As I wasn't allowed to take any of my medicines when I got back to my house I had to contact my doctor as my system was in shock and she wanted to know what was wrong, when I told her what happened she could not believe it and placed me under watch because I showed signs of cabin fever but not the type that you have to get out of the cabin but instead that I had to stay in. It is technically called withdrawing from society. I could have cared less.

The fact that I had a private attorney, and I was getting out, was the saving grace. The whole out come was that I was allowed to have this sealed because I never did anything before or after this. Please tell me what I did differently from what they really do, and why are they not in trouble ??????? THEY are the ones protecting YOU!!!!!!!!!!!! THINK ABOUT IT!!!!!!!!!!! Will You for they really get away with mur_____ what do you think?????

I am disabled now because of my health when I think of what they did it really ties me up and makes me very sick to my stomach. Believe me it still goes on even now. Just because they got me out doesn't mean that they didn't find some other poor sole to do this to.

My boyfriend came to me and said "He wanted to get married. He wanted to meet my sisters and finally settled down with me. This was going to happen in the year of 2000." I had my house and he had his. I put mine up for sale and it sold immediately. His has not sold yet. He told me that "He wanted to be with me and he wanted to spend the rest of our lives together. Well, after the years we have been together, and what had happened that's really what I wanted as well." I now do not have my house.

My boyfriend does not believe that if we got married that I could separate my family from us. Boy He really doesn't know me very well. When someone does something like this to me, believe me I really don't care if I ever see them again in my life, this one or the next. I am resorting to having to live in a-one room efficiency and thank God for this gentleman named Sal that I ran into today. I will take the efficiency and do what I have to do in order to make it through.

I can not get a house as I can not qualify for a house at this time. Funny, I used to have a four bedroom house. I helped people and let them stay at my place and now, it's really an inconvenience for them to let me stay at theirs. Well I will do what I have to and just ask God to be on my side to watch out for me. I'm not a religious fanatic but he is out there for us.

# CHAPTER 13

RECENTLY THERE WAS A county commissioner that was in trouble and I don't know the entire allegation and the situations about his circumstances. However, if I may I will use a passage that he kept saying "That when the powers that be want to get you, they'll get you." Oh, that is oh so true and there is absolutely nothing you can do about it, and you are the innocent party.

I went back to get my belongings from my sisters house and we had a very heated discussion. We have come to a very serious conclusion that we just cannot live together and if we want to get together and go to a movie or meet and go to dinner, well that would be different. Living together that is out of the question.

We have met and had dinner together and that is good.

We are all in the situation from hurricane Katrina. My best friend was killed in a car accident today, Monday, and I was not aware of this. It is now Thursday, and Katrina hits the US. Friday morning, I am at a friends store and I get a phone call on my cell from my friend's sister. She calls me to tell me that my best friend was killed in a car accident on Monday along with her 10 year old son. I absolutely could not believe this.

I have known her for 35 years. We grew up together since we were in the 6th grade. I got the call that a friend needed to speak to me in reference to an emergency, before I knew it was about my girlfriend that was killed. I started calling everybody I knew to find out who it could be. When the call came in as to who it was, I was devastated.

My sister told me she would take me to the funeral as she did not think I should drive because she didn't feel that I could handle the drive to the funeral. I thought that was nice of her, so I told her I would pay for the gas if she took me. When I got to the funeral home, I saw my friend's sister and I could not believe that it was oh so true that my best friend was actually gone. I can never call her again and ask her to do the things we used to do.

The realization had set in and I was truly upset. I had missed her little brother and I would have to wait to see him until the next day. I needed to see him too. I had to go to the casket and see my best friend. Wahoo!!!!!! I couldn't walk up there. My knees would not let me do it. I was going down fast. Somebody was behind me picking me up and I had no idea who it was. It was one of the guys we went to school with. I had not seen him since senior high.

The next day was the funeral and my sister said "She would drive me to the funeral". I said "Okay." My other girlfriend also came with me. My other girlfriends name is Colet. She sat next to me and as they placed my girlfriend Sue's pictures on the screens I started crying. I am sorry I could not help that as I grew up with her since I was eleven years old. My sister then sitting next to Colet said "Lee-Ann Do I have to take you out of the church? Or do you want to go to the back of the church as everyone is looking at you.

Excuse me but I was not hysterically crying or out of line. When father asked if anyone else had anything to say about Sue and Jack, I raised my hand and I got up and spoke. I said "I know that everybody here today has known Sue for long periods of time and I would not take that away from any of you. I also have known her for a long period of time. We used to be at each others houses and she was eleven months younger than I. She was the younger sister I never had. We did everything together. When my mother passed, Sue was there and no questions were asked. When her father passed I was there and no questions were asked. When her mother passed I was there no questions were asked. My sister's statement was due to my red face which I did not under stand at the time. Her statement was because she was worried for me that maybe I was in CHF again. And did not know what to do for me.

Today are Christmas Day and her husband called me asking me to come over and help him get through the day? He said "he could not make it through the day without me because it was too hard to remember the Christmas past without them". That it was the first Christmas without them. He went to the Cemetery and then we met at the house. I did not want to go to the cemetery as I truly wanted to remember her as she was. I have been her friend for so long that she is always in my heart and that's where she will remain. We spent the day together and had dinner and then I went home. We will spend New Year's Eve together this year.

When Sue had a tat with her first boyfriend and she needed to move out, she called me up and I went over to her house and I packed her up and just moved her out. When Jack was born and she changed his diaper for the first time, and he peed on the ceiling she called me and we started laughing saying "How do you change little boy's diapers quickly without getting baths?" Sue I will always love you. I miss you honey.

Now my sister calls me up to tell me that I am a great Aunt again. However when I ask what hospital the mother and father and child were at, I am told that I should not go visit there because they need to bond because they only have a little bit of time to do this, and then he must go back to a facility. Well I am on a tight schedule as well and she is quite aware of this too. So that works out quite well.

Sometimes you wonder if people actually listen to themselves when they say the things they say, and act the way they do. It all comes back to them one way or another. I met someone who asked me to sit and write this book. As I sit here and write it, I can not get hold of him in order to publish it. I suppose I would have to get a hold of another publisher.

I am at the store and all of a sudden here comes a big yellow school bus. Well I thought it was for the little school next door. Then here comes thirty school kids and they all pile out of the bus and sit on the side walk very orderly. Then the counselors came in and gave me there orders. After I took the order and sat with the kids for a few minutes,

I said "I really enjoyed this and I must take a picture of this and your school bus. For No one will ever believe me unless I have a picture of this." After they left I called the boss and said "Oh by the way did you forget to tell me something?" He said "yes, by the way, there will be a big school bus coming by." I said "too late boss, they were all ready here with thirty kids and a few counselors. I already took care of them but next time how about a heads up?" He said "okay."

Well occasionally we will get the local dogs that come with the owners that he would give a small cup of ice cream to and it was very cute. They would come on the three sided scooters. You know the kind that has the car on the side and the scooter is the main part. They would come beside the horses. They come in the cars, in the back of the pick up trucks. They all love there ice cream cones.

I have all kinds of animals that come for Ice cream. I have all kinds of animals that like my ice cream. I have a family of three dogs that come religiously to get there ice cream. There names are Jenny, Noel, and Wilmer. Jenny is a Shepard and she eats hers very cordially. Noel is a lab and he wastes no time to eat his ice cream. Wilmer is a beagle and he follows Noel in wasting no time. It's funny that they know me and wait for me to feed them there ice cream. Then here comes the horses. The girls were standing eating the cones and the horses just reached over the girls shoulders and ate the girl's ice cream cones.

I could not believe this so I went back inside and made the girl's another cone and grabbed my camera so I could take pictures of the horses because no one again would believe me if I told them that the horses were eating ice cream cones from the girls. We have such fun with the animals and they are so special that I thanked the girl's for sharing those moments with me. I have quite a few that bring the horses up for carrot cones if they don't allow them to have ice cream I make them a carrot cone.

Well I took a sixteen day European trip. I went to Italy, Rome, Spain, Germany, Holland, Switzerland, and England. We landed in Heathrow and took the double-decker bus to the hotel, got up the next morning and started our tour bus. I only had sixteen people on my tour bus. That was interesting the number of people to the number of days on the tour. We started out in Rome and saw the coliseum and ruins and then we went to the Cathedrals.

We went shopping and saw the sea of the blue on blue. Where the blue sky meets the blue sea and it literally looks like no separation between the earth and the sky. It is a beautiful sight. Then we went to Holland and saw the Windmills and the tulip fields which were astonishing. They took us to a cheese factory, and showed us how to make cheese and I could not eat cheese for quite some time after that.

I literally got sick after seeing this. We would stop by a lot of the fruit stands because my tour guide would say "okay I know that Lee Ann likes a lot of fruit so this one is just for you. Let' get out and stretch and get some fruit." It was great.

Then we went to Switzerland and we were in the Alps and it was beautiful. The mountain tops had snow on it and the temperature was lovely. Not to cold and not to hot. We went to a little casino and played the machines. They didn't have big tables just a few machines. Then we went to folklore at night. It was very nice. Then we went on a canoe ride. The next morning we went to Spain. It was a lot of fun.

We had to take a boat to get to it. We strolled out on the gondolas through the city. They had a parade in the city in the afternoon and we were watching it. That was very nice. We would watch the mimics show in the court yard. Now we are back on the boat to go to Italy.

We are on the bus and going through the hillside back to Rome. We are driving through and we are at a check point where we can not get off the bus but our passports must be stamped. Our tour guide gets them stamped and we just stay on the bus. We are all playing a game on the bus. We all get along great. We are going to take a ride on the Vine.

It is a boat ride on the side of the mountain where they make the wine. You can see the castles. There are quite a few of these here on this vine. We are getting a little taste tester as we go through the vine as well. Now we must take the bus back toward Rome. We are riding around toward this castle and you can get out and walk in it. It is beautiful. We are walking through the mount. You can actually see the gate that was placed in it hundreds of years ago and we are going through this room that has a beautiful painting on the walls. You are not allowed to take pictures and that is what preservers the painting. If you stand on the balcony you can see the city below. We are now heading toward Germany.

This is truly beautiful the grass is green that it looks like it was painted on the ground. The auto bound train goes by so fast that you feel that you just blinked and you missed something. I guess you did if you didn't watch it the first, second or two. We are going to go to the Castles of Germany. There are so many. We will also go to the watch maker. I found this little shop that had the nicest little gifts.

One was a replica of a piano and one was a horn and my nice and nephew played these instruments, so I bought these those for them. The castles had these figurines on them that were the size life. When you looked up at them you looked like you were looking at a human being. If you looked at them too long you could get a kink in your neck. There were a lot of castles in this country. Now we are headed back to Rome.

We are back at Rome and we are going to the see the City under the city. We are going to see the little boy who runs away from mom. We are going to see the wishing well at night that is lit up. This is a sight to see, the water fall that comes up around the well is something to see. Then we are going to have a little party. Tomorrow we are going to go to the Vatican. They showed us the seven year door. When you walk into the Vatican you see a lot of murals an altar and there are paintings. There are tombs of popes from pasts in glass. You will walk around a gold altar. You go downstairs and there are more tombs of popes. This is like walking through a grave yard of popes.

Then you walk into the court yard into the sixteen chapels. This is the biggest and most beautiful mural I have ever seen. You are not allowed to take a picture of this as it is so old the flash will disincarnate the tapestry because of the age. You can take a picture of the mural of paint and this is at the end. Then there are the statues that are partially broken that are still standing.

This is amazing that these pieces are still standing centuries and centuries later and they never had the machinery that we have to make these statues. We are going to go to dinner and a show this evening. We are getting off the bus and the other bus driver almost hit me. I went to step off the bus and the other driver just pulled up and did not look.

My bus driver jumped off the bus and pushed me out of the way and started cussing him out in French. I was so shuck up that the shows dealer came out and gave us the show for free. That was very nice of them however that bus driver was ridiculous.

The next morning we all went out to our last breakfast together and went to the airport to go back to our lives wherever they took us. We were from America, South Africa, and Brazil. That was the one of the best trips I ever took. I usually take trips by myself. Bob has never taken a foreign trip with me. I hope we do some day.

I take trips now and meet Bob on the road. We meet and go to Georgia. Sometimes we meet and go to South Carolina. I drove up to South Carolina once. I was going to look at a Dairy Queen that I was going to purchase but my car was not working correctly and I had to get back to my mechanic to get it fixed so I could not make the trip to see if it was what I wanted. I will make it to see if that is what I want sooner or later.

Well I am driving and my truck still feels like it is not running right. Bob is with me and it feels like it a Mack truck. He tells me that "he would not drive it. He would get a rental and leave it with the mechanic until it was fixed." I said "honey that would be a lot easier for you because you are not handicapped and you do not have to have handicap equipment in your car. Remember, I drive with a left foot gas pedal in my car." He said "Oh I forgot about that thing. Why can't you drive a regular car for a couple of days?" I said "because I can't feel the gas pedal so I don't know if I am pressing the gas or the break and I would not know if it were down to the floor or not. It is not easy to get a vehicle with handicap equipment."

So I called him up to day and asked him to meet me for a little afternoon delight. We have been together for so long that we go hand in glove together. I will call him up and leave him little messages about love letters on his phone. I would get one the plane today and be in the suitcase today to be there with him forever and never look back.

Let's go for sky ride and take a sky dive to the wild winds. Walk in the water falls and make love on a sandy beach on a moon lit night. As we are making love in the duns of the cave with the water falls below and the whisper of the water flowing talking to us as we make love. How beautiful the moves of the ways. To be with the one you love.

Now it is our time to open another restaurant in another city. We will call it Curls and Touches. We have been in the business so long and know how to do this so we can make it work now. We have a sitter for the baby and while he is still young we can get ground work done on the restaurant. This way when we have to be at the restaurant we will be there as much as needed. We can put in as many hours as needed and she can stay with the baby. I will have a room for parties. I think I will put a big screen TV so you can watch ball games. Then you can book a party in advance. You can have little parties for little ones too. I will have cakes made upon requests for these occasions.

At this point I had gotten into another accident and I was not at fault. My girlfriend told me that I could come and rent a room with her until I was to go and be with Bob. We are planning to be together by the end of the year. I stayed with her until September when her sister was arrested for drug charges.

Her sister had her oldest son with her at the time of her arrest who was arrested as well. This left her other three kids with no where to go. Lou was going to take care of them in January but now that her sister was arrested she had to take them earlier, so this left me with being put out of my room earlier than originally planned. Now I had to find another place to live. I have a friend who said "she needed a room mate and I could stay there and help her with her son at first." I tried to help her with her son, however that did not work.

Now I am just living at her house. I assume that I will be going with Bob but I am not sure of the date. Louis is now taking care of the kids and their names are David, Tasha, and Charles. David is giving her a lot of grief. He does not like to listen and she is having a very hard time with him. I think he might end up like his father and older brother because he thinks it's cute and that they are all just fine. It must be pretty cool to sit your butt in a jail cell and do nothing but drugs all your life rather than make something out of it.

# CHAPTER 19

ALTHOUGH HE WORKS PART time now and likes it, he wants to send some money to his father for commissary. Louis does not like it when he sends it to him but she really can not say anything to him because he will do it behind her back if she does. Tasha is very good. She works part time as well. She loves to work and make some money. She does not want to send money to her parents. She does not want to talk to them. She does not want to see them. She does not agree with what they did. She knows the difference between what they did and what Louis is trying to do for her and accepts this as a good thing however David will not take this.

Now there is Charles, he is moldable. He wants to do well by Louis and wants to hang with his big brother as well. He doesn't want to listen to Louis too well and he wants to act like his big brother. On the other hand he want's to please Louis so he can make her proud of him, as he realizes that she is the only one that took him and his sister and brother and would do what she is doing for them. Now I sat down with him and told him "that he should appreciate Aunt Louis a little more than just giving her a lot of headaches and heartaches and he should do as she asks because she did not have to take them into her home and care for them as she did.

She could have let them go into a foster home and then they would never be in the same home and see each other again. If they though they had it tough at Aunt Louis's house they should learn to appreciate what she was doing and one day they would truly love her for the things that she is doing. They should ask there cousins Pep and Sally about the times that they lived in my house with me and see if I was not correct in what I was saying."

My medicines are so expensive that I can not afford to pay for them. I do not know what to do at times. My pharmacist jokes with me whether I am eating or paying for my medicine however at times it is the truth because a box of cereal goes a long way. I wonder "if the president would feel the same way if he had to do the same thing? Does he really understand what it is to make a decision on whether it is to eat or take medicine because you can not afford it?"

The TV commercials may have used this as an advertisement to get you to vote for a candidate however when you are in this position it really is not funny. How about the older persons who eat dog food and cat food in the cans because it is cheaper and they can then afford the med's they need. Well I guess I will go have to find a part time job again just to pay for my medicine and see if I can make it that way.

Bob used to own a restaurant. I could run it while he was on the road if he would help me start up the restaurant. I could manage it and be there and he could come by when he came back in town. It would be some what like the one he used to have. I would change it a little. I would make sure that you could book "football parties, and special occasions parties something I know that his restaurant never did." I have a lot of ideas that would go off very well once I get it started.

I would have an office dinner drawing party that would allow your office to receive a discount for lunch or dinner in order to bring in my local customers. These things are just a few of the things that I would work on to enhance my clientele that I know that were not done in the previous restaurant.

I would have so much fun getting this restaurant together and working it that I would not have time to be bored or argue with him and I know that it would only make our relationship better.

We never argue or fuss at each other. It is extremely hard that both of us are apart from one another now and that we are not in the same state. I miss him so and he misses me. We talk on the phone and the loneliness that is in his voice I know he will never admit to it but I know that man like no other person. He is very lonely now and there is no one else that can fulfill this spot in his heart. I am his soul mate and he his mine. I tell him this and I also tell him that I don't want anyone else to fill this spot in my heart only I can.

I may be standing making a sandwich for a customer and it may be the type of sandwich that he likes to eat and I will be thinking about what is he doing, where is he, is he okay? Then I may be thinking oh my, my panties are wet just thinking about him, this is ridiculous. After these many years this man still does this to me. Just the thought of him touching me and the way he does makes me this way. You think you are over a man? You can walk away from him? But no.

He says he thinks about me and he is hard and he can't walk around. He can't get out of his car. He can't move away from his desk because it is ridiculous. That is because he is thinking about me and the way I touch him and what I do for him. Can he walk away from me? Is he still in love with me? Are we still soul mates? We have been together for twenty-seven years. We love each other dearly. Would you not say?

I would pack all my things and leave tomorrow to go and be with Bob. I would leave everything here and go. I have nothing holding me back. If he says that he wants to be together this weekend then my guys that fix my truck said "they would drive my truck up there so that if it were to break down on the way they could fix it." They said that "if I were to go this weekend they would put a hitch on the back of my truck and move all my things up there with a u-haul and then come back on a motor cycle." This way they could have a road trip and a break so that they could know that I was safe.

They said that they wanted to deliver me to him so that they knew that I was safe. They know that I know how to drive to Georgia and meet him there because I have driven that road trip so many times to see him. I also go and visit my sister in Georgia so I have taken this road a few other times.

Bob and I have so many beliefs that are the same that it is not funny. When it comes to the baby we believe in a lot of disciplinary factors that we think the baby should have that are similar. He said to me "honey, it's scary that we think so much alike when it comes to discipline of the baby, and how we want to raise the baby. We should not have any problem raising him because we both think so much alike." You have to wonder why there is any doubt that we would not be good together.

I am staying at a friend's house and she has a twelve year old son. He is not too easy to handle. He thinks he does not have to listen to any one. This is worse than a typical twelve year old kid. He needs a good swift kick in the rump. Something he probably never got when he was a young kid. Now it's too late. Maybe not if it was done right. You have to stand over him like a sergeant at arms in the army or something to have him do what you want done.

He doesn't like it to well and then throws a temper tantrum. He will storm out of the house and run away to a neighbor's house and call his mom on her cell phone to tell her where he is. Then just before it is his bed times he comes back home and will not say anything to you as to where he went or what he did. So he thinks he has the upper hand in all this but he does not as his mom tells me where he went the next morning. So when he goes to the school, she tells the counselor and they take care of the situation at school. He is in a special military school for troubled kids.

When I first came to stay with them I was to watch him and help him with his home work. I asked him to go for a walk one night to show me the neighborhood. He took me on a walk that was so long that I had trouble walking back as I have a broken leg, and I wear a brace on my right foot. We started off out of the front door and were going to go to the Tom Tomb store. We walked up by the expressway and over the expressway down to the shopping center and around the complex. Then we had to walk around the back of the complex. When we got into the front of the complex he bolted in and ran to the house.

As I did not know what street I was to turn on I was lost. I took my phone with me and I called him. Then I said "Tom now that you are home take your medicine, take a shower, and go to bed." When I finally got there he came down and asked me what took me so long? I said "if I wasn't lost I would have found my way a little faster but being that you thought it necessary to leave me and get me lost, it took me a little longer to find my way home. So do as I told you to do and go to bed. He had the phone in his hand and I took it out of his hand and he said "what are you doing" and I said "I did not say you could talk on the phone. That was not one of the things I told you to do."

He did not like it to well but he went to bed and did not give me a hard time about this. He told his mom the next morning. She was not happy with him about him leaving me in the neighborhood alone not knowing where I was because something could have happened to me and nobody would have known who I was or where I was staying. Nobody around here knows who I am.

I was trying to get Lou to get David into military school as it would help him before he has trouble like his parents and his brother, but lately she has not had any time for me. I call her and she can never meets with me to have breakfast so I can't talk to her about anything. I don't know what she will do with him. She will call one day and I will be busy and not be able to meet with her and I'm sure she will not like that too well. Maybe she will see how it feels when you always disregard your friends that you have had for years and years. However, maybe she wants too.

I am staying with some friends and I am safe now. It is truly funny that through all of this not once at any time did Bob say "Honey, come and stay with me." This is my boyfriend. He is supposed to be my all of everything to me, my heart and soul. I sold my house to get married to him and then we were going to adopt a child remember? Well he adopted a child and now I am being told that now that he is a parent "he does not no what he wants."

He says "that things have changed and he is not sure of what to do. That he can not tell me if we are going to be together and that it is not necessarily to important if he has a girlfriend or a wife or mother for his son to help him raise his child." WOW this is the thanks and the relationship he has given me after twenty-seven years of being with him, and after meeting with him on the road and trying to make the relationship work so that neither one of us would be alone all rest of our lives.

I told him that it is only fair that he makes up his mind and makes a decision as to what he wants, because it is not fair to keep me hanging on and making me lose everything I broke my back for all my life. I want to get back on my feet either with or without him and if he can keep discarding me then he can do it once and for all. He left me twice before so if he found it that easy before than he can find it that easy now.

His friend says "He was working his way back to me with a burning love inside." If that is true then when I am being put out on the street and you are trying to work your way back to me, wouldn't you say "okay sweetie come and stay with me no matter where you are." No matter where your boss sends you to live? Would it really take so long to say "Okay come and be with me?" I told him that if he ever lost his house he would never have been homeless because he could have always came and stayed with me. However I can not say the same for him because he did not ever say that to me and this came up in a conversation about being homeless.

I told him that the next time I get a home I would not lose it again. No matter where it was or who it was with. It did not matter how I got it or when I get it, I will not lose it one more time. I told him that I will not be homeless one more time in my life. As I struggled from a two bedroom apartment that was less than one bedroom of a regular house made into a garage apartment for eight years and I washed my dishes in the shower I cooked on a Bunsen burner and a toaster oven. Then I bought my first house. Then I bought my second house and then my third. Now I do not have one and I sold it to be with Bob and all I get is that I am changing and I do not know if I want the same things. I told him that he better think long and hard before he says that it is over. Once he says "it's over, he has no idea how much I mean it and he will soon find out the hard way."

As I have been in three car accidents since 2002 and not one of them was my fault. This has caused me some serious problems. I have always had a house and always had room for anyone who needed it. I added a room so that we had an extra room to accommodate more people, in order so as not to have to turn people out. I remember being told that I would not be put out. Yet here I am out in the streets so to say and guess what, it's by the same one that said I would not be there. The next house I get I will not loose again I will guarantee you that.

Bob and I in our fairy tale relationship, adopted the child and have come to the status that he has the baby and since he is the parent he has changed. Now, he is not sure of what he wants. He does not know if he wants us to be together. We meet in Georgia or in Skyburst but I have not been in Minnesota with him. It truly makes me upset that he will not keep his promise that we were suppose to be together and raise the baby. What happened to "honey we think so much alike and we have the same beliefs about raising the baby?"

He just wants to make up so many excuses for reasons that we are not together and I am suppose to just take them all in. What about the times when he left me and married other women and I am just suppose to forget them? I'm just supposing to look the other way and act like those things have never happened and yet he has the nerve to compare them with me. How dare he expect me to except comparison of his wives?

I told him that whether it was with or without him I was going to spend the rest of my life with someone. I did not want to be alone. I did not want to be living in one state and him in another. If I wanted to be alone I would have chosen to be that way a long time ago. I would have never sold my house just to be alone and if he never intended to be with me why did he go to each one of my sisters and ask them if he could marry me, if he did not want to do so?

It was not fair that I have given up my home for him and now I have nothing and he has a place, yet he will not make up his mind if he will let me go or not. I do not want to be kept on hanging on a string any longer. Four years is long enough to make up your mind whether or not you want to have me by your side. We have been together longer than that but the last four you finally ask my sisters if you could marry me.

You never met my father and mother and now you can not meet my mom but you can still meet my father. I knew your dad, and I know your mom. I know most of your friends and you know most of mine. You are going through some tough medical times and you won't let me be there with you and this is upsetting as you don't always talk. I have to pull these conversations out of you at times. Sometimes it is like talking to a brick wall. You don't call me at night and tell me how your day went. You don't send me flowers. You don't send me a card. Yet you got mad at me when I sent you a monkey in a jail telling you to "RESCUE ME" and a card. Oh then there was the time when I sent you the panties and you wanted to know if they were wet because of me wearing them or if they were scented.

I told you to smell them and find out if you could not tell and if you did not think I would send you something to remind you of me and to open in private. Then there is the issue of I don't even have his address at this time in his life. What is up with that? I know that he lives in Minnesota but I can not tell you where because he does not want to give me an address.

He had a problem with his tags on his vehicles about two years ago. He said "honey, I am having a big problem with the registration on the vehicles and no-one can get it straighten out." I said "why?" He said" I don't know" I said "give me the registration and the lease agreement the insurance, a copy of all paperwork on the car and a letter giving me the right to pick up the tags and I will go down to the tag agency and get your tags."

So I took the paper work and I went down to the tag agency and with all this information and they said that "I needed a power of attorney from him and he lives in another state." I called him and "he told me to sign it" I did and brought it back in and they gave me the tag I then called him and asked him if he wanted me to send it to him or wait and bring it up to him as we were going to meet in about two weeks anyway.

He told me to wait and he would get it in two weeks. When I went to bring the tag to him he could not believe that I got it done so quickly because the person in North Carolina could not get the tags. I asked "Why not is it because maybe she wanted to go out with you and maybe you would not go out with her? Or maybe you just would not give her all the paperwork that I made you give me? It does not matter it is over and done.

# CHAPTER 20

WELL TODAY I HAD a doctor's appointment and you will never believe who I ran into in the doctor's office. Do you remember the girl Bobbie who accused me of having an affair with my Sgt in the DUI tape room? Of all the people to run into I had to run into her today. She truly would not sit next to me in the waiting area which was okay with me because I had nothing to say to her. That is her guilty complex that is talking to her about what she did to me that would not allow her to talk to me. I said "Hello to her but I did not have anything else to say." The doctor says "I may be going back into Congestive Heart Failure" because I have gained fifteen pounds of water and I can not get it off. I am having trouble releasing it and it is not from the food I am eating.

She wants me to go back to the Cardiologist and see if there is something else going on and what to do about it. This is before I wind up back in the hospital. Bob told me that he was in the hospital for chest pains just recently. He did not understand what they were from. He also has Diabetes. I wonder if he thinks that I am going to keep taking him back on his whimper and wimps every time he thinks that he can run away. I told him to make up his mind whether or not he wants us to be together or not and now it is Thanksgiving and of course were not together.

I love him dearly but I am not just a sex toy for him, sometimes that is how it feels just meeting him on the road and only spending time with him there and not having a life with him any other way. He left me for other women and then has the nerve to compare me with them. Well I guess telling him that I need a solid answer whether we are going to be together is going to let him know that I truly mean business, that I do love him and that he can commit to me once and for all or leave me alone. If this should scare him then he needs to take a good long hard look at the road he chose to take with the baby by himself.

He would come to the Dairy Queen and want to have a rondavue in the Bathroom. This would turn him on and then he wanted me to meet him in the hotel room and finish him off. He would say that it excited him to have me touch him in the bathroom and then meet him in the hotel room afterwards. When we met on the road he would call me and ask me where I was and to see how far I was or to see if I was in an accident. That was sweet and considerate.

He is in that manner. We would go to dinner and go back to the Hotel room. Sometimes it is okay and other times it would be nice to go to a movie and then go back to the hotel room. Not just run back to the Hotel room. I really don't care how long we have been seeing each other. It has a tendency to get on your nerves. I don't care who you are. I am sure you would like to be in a normal relationship.

I had to file for personal Bankruptcy and was awarded it by the court at which time one of my creditors that was placed on the schedule decided to file a judgment against me. The judgment filed by them was illegal because it was placed on me the day after I was awarded my bankruptcy. I sent this information to the credit bureaus and asked their assistance in getting it removed and I received help from only one. The other two would not assist me in releasing this information so I had to get an attorney to get this job done.

Due to one of the accidents I was in I suffer seizures from. I was in an attorney's office when I had a seizure. I was speaking to him and they thought that I was made at them. I told them that I was not made at them but that I was having a seizure and that I could not talk at the time. When the seizure was over I would be glad to answer any questions for them. They asked me "how often do they come on? When did they start? Is there anything that makes them come on? Have I seen a doctor? Am I on medicine for these?" I said "there was no certain time for them to come on, and they started about six months ago".

There is nothing particularly for me to do that would make this start. "Yes, I have seen a doctor and I am taking medicine. I can not afford the medicine as it is five hundred dollars a bottle and I must take three hundred milligrams a day." I am currently getting help from the doctor's office with the medicine. I am trying to get on the patient assistance program.

I am working part time with some kids at subway. I have a crew of kids whose names are Mars, Lars, Nicole, Princes, Trish, Mike, Carlito, and Money. Lars, Princes, Trish and Money are my best friends. Money and I were making subs one day for a football game for his school. We made five hundred six inch subs of tuna, chicken breast, and turkey. We had this done in a matter of three hours. I was cutting the bread and placing the meat in the bread and Money would put the lettuce on the sandwich and wrap it. Then mark each one as to what kind of sandwich it was so that the school would know when they got it and they would not be confused on the field.

Everybody said "we did a wonderful job." We did not get one complaint out of that big job. Our boss was very proud of us. Money and I still work together as all the others and we have a great time. Carlito and I work together very well. He is a great kid. We work like butter, very smooth. We start the prep work together and then start the customers together. We start the cleaning together. We work hand in hand. He's a great kid.

Today is Thanksgiving and I am spending it with a friend. My family has not even had the decency to call and ask me to come to diner. I call to say Happy Thanksgiving and I refuse to let them know how much it hurts inside that they just keep stabbing the knife in deeper and deeper each time. You see when you don't do anything, why are you the one left out in the cold?

Yet when the next holidays come around it doesn't make it any easier to want to be around them. I have a sister in another state and that one would offer me the time to be with her. I would take the drive if my body could physically take it. The last time I tried to take such a drive I was in such pain and misery that I could not stand to do anything. I was going to a baby shower and I had to miss the shower because the drive was too long.

It truly hurts thou when you take the kids when they are little every where and now that they are big and have there own, they are not decent enough to ask you to dinner and spend the time with you on the Holidays. I just have to get through the day and I will be okay and strong today for tomorrow when I wake I hope that I will be stronger in my heart for the pain that is caused today. I think of the things we used to do when we were little and it truly hurts that they treat me this way now that we are older.

When I was a little girl my father used to say "he was tired of listening to US yelling that I could not turn the jump rope over my sister's shoulders because my shoulders hurt me to much. I had no idea that I had arthritis in my shoulders so bad. He took my mothers old mixers and made an electric jump rope out of them. He made a box and put the motor in it. He took a clowns head and put the rope coming out of the mouth so it would turn the rope. Then he made two tripods one for one end and one for the other end.

You would put them apart for the distance of the height of the person you were trying to jump the rope. Then turn it on. Bingo, you have a jump rope. Besides if you wanted to do it by yourself, you could do it by yourself. You did not need three people.

I was walking in the toy store the other day looking for a special toy for a toping to decorate a cake. About forty years ago my father invented an electric jump rope. He had it patented and he could not afford to have it mass produced. He took my mother to China to see if a toy company (Mattel Toy Co.) would be interested in producing this toy. They said "it would never make it on the market."

I walked pass this certain toy and it caught my eye. You would never guess what it was. Yes, it was an Electric Jump Rope! Of all things. My father's invention was now on the market by somebody else Mattel. I could not believe what I was seeing. I got the information down on paper and wanted to contact these people and find out how this could be. It was his invention and he should have the rights. He said "it didn't matter. Your mother is dead and gone and she could not wreak the profits form it so I did not worry about the legal ramifications of it being on the market." I said "What about us girls. Wouldn't you fight for us? After all Dads there are six of us?" He said "if I wanted to I could but he could not fight it as he is too old."

Some of the other crazy things that we did when we were little were drinking from a garden hose and not from bottled water. We shared one soft drink with four friends, form one bottle and not one actually died from this imagine. We ate cupcakes, white bread and real butter and drank koolade made with sugar, but we weren't overweight because we were always outside playing. We would leave home in the morning and play all day, as long as we were back when the street lights came on.

No one was able to reach us all day. And we were O.K. We would spend hours building go carts out of scraps and then ride down the hill, only to find out we forgot the brakes. After running into the bushes a few times, we learned to solve the problems. We did not have Play stations, Nintendo's, X-boxes, no video games at all, no 150 channels on cable video movies or DVD's, no surround-sound or CD's, no cell phones, no personal computers, no internet chat rooms......

We were given BB guns for our 10th birthday, made up games with sticks and tennis balls and, an eye never came out. We were told it could happen but we did not put out any eyes. We rode bikes or walked to a friend's house and knocked on the door or rang the bell, or just walked in and talked to them!

Little league had tryouts and not everyone made the team. Those who didn't had to learn to deal with disappointment. Imagine that! The idea of a parent bailing us out if we broke the law was unheard of. They actually sided with the Law.

We used to pick wild berries from the fields of all kinds next to us when they were in bloom. Mother knew where we were because we would bring these big buckets of berries back home. Then we bring home buckets of pears and apples from the field across the street from us. We always had fun doing this. It wasn't like it was work when we were picking these.

We used to make these huge forts out of snow in the winter and just pick up the top layer of snow. Then you would place the top layer of the snow on the rolls of snow and you could make a fort or an igloo to sit in and it would keep the wind from blowing around you. I remember we were doing this one year and the dog was with us and she thought the ice was hard enough so she went on the pool and instead of her walking on the ice she fell in the water and all of a sudden you heard her yelping.

My girlfriend Louis said to me "that she wishes that she had me at her house because she misses me there and she misses our time together. That the kids are misbehaving and that she can not control them. She may have to let the State take control of the as they are too much for her. She said that "she is sorry that I left the house because at least when I was there she had her sanity and she could do what she wanted and she knew that her bills would be paid. I gave her rent money and it was never late. The kids refuse to do what they are suppose to do and will not listen to her."

I have been kicked out of living quarters too many times and the next time I move it will be for the last time I move. I will only move to put a roof over my head that I am going to buy myself or that I may be going to be with Bob, if that is whom I am to be with. Maybe I am to meet someone else in this life and be with someone else who can treat me like a lady and respect me. Maybe I will meet someone who cares about me and is not so selfish. It is truly hard in this world when you love someone and they say they love you but they treat you like this.

I thought that Bob was that special person but his comments and attitude lately have been quite a bit much. Now that he is a parent and that is the child that we were to have adopted together and raise I have truly not even met yet. The baby will be one years old soon and I would like to see what he is going to do. I wonder if we are going to be together or not? I wish I could meet someone that I could spend the rest of my life with that would just appreciate me for me and not be so selfish about it.

Today is Thanksgiving and he has not even called me. Not even to wish me a Happy Thanksgiving. That's not right. I called him and he did not pick up the phone. He says "now that he has the baby he does not pick the phone up after six pm. Does he think the world stops because he has a child after six pm?" I hate to tell him that it does not. It continues to go on and that it can function and people still live even though a child is in the house. That's a little hard to swallow.

Now that a child is in the house it should be more exciting. It should be coming home and having fun with the baby. We should be looking forward to doing things with the baby. Going places with him and reading to him. Watching him grow and discovering all his first little things that he learns together. I wonder what the two of them are doing now. Are they having fun?

Is he laughing and has he started to walk yet? Bob told me that he started him in a walker and that he only started to walk backwards, so I told him to start pulling him forward so that he would get the idea that he is to start walking forward. He said "that's an idea." I went "no s h t Sherlock that's the way you teach them to walk if they are having difficulty figuring it out by themselves. You have to give them incentives as to what they are to do in order to let them know. That is what teaching them truly all is about."

About a year ago I met someone and he would come into the store and leave me five dollars in my tip jar. He would then keep asking me "if I was going to give it up?" Was I going to let him have some of me? What is this, just because he wanted to leave me five dollars tip he thought he had the right to ask if he could have sex with me? Get out of here he does not even know me. He never even took me out to coffee. I don't just hop into bed with someone.

He can definitely go a house further. I ran into him on Thanksgiving Day and he asked me "where I was spending the day?" I said "at a friend's house." He said "so are you going to give it up yet?" I just looked at him and shook my head in discuss. What is wrong with these people? Are there not any more decent men out there?

You sit and wonder if any of these people these days have any morals or values to themselves or for anybody else. There does not appear to be anything like dating any more or is it because they just meat you they expect that you have to "give it up" with out getting to even know you! How rude or even discussing is this. All I could even think or feel like was oh my goodness the feeling of harassment from the police department all over again after ten years of this nonsense. That was a bit much. It really burned me I suppose more than I realized.

Now this is to really get you after all we have been through together so far we are going to go through some more now. I am currently going through a blockage in my heart upon exertion I will loose my breath and it gets real ugly. I am now carrying nitro, let's just shorten that for now. At least as a joke that's the shortest part of the shortness we can deal with. Ha Ha! Seriously I am going to the cardiologist and they are all putting there heads together to figure out what happened. They are investigation the best course of action to take. It's all in God's hands anyway so what ever will be will be and let the powers of him be and the cardiologists will do the right thing.

You know I wanted to open a restaurant for myself in another state but with this I can not do this. I will have to wait and see what will happen with the doctors first. I started by investing with a company and I only hope that I can get it back. If I can not get the money back I truly will be sick to my stomach to have to save this money all over again. It took everything I had to do it in the first place and I will do it again but I truly hope I can get it back.

Well I am told that I will get it back and thank goodness that I can because that would truly give me a heart attack if I could not get it back. I am at Dairy Queen today and it is truly very slow. This new owner is unbelievable. She thinks that she needs to play this child's games by writing you up and that this is going to settle with you after you have worked at this store for so long.

I am not going to sign these papers and if this is required I will walk out and she can find someone else to work in my place. It is not as if the place has been so popping like it used to be before she bought it anyway. A lot of my customers want to know if I leave where I will go because they say they will follow me where ever I go they won't stay here. They only come here for me, not for her.

Today is Thursday and it is about 08:30 in the morning. Bob calls and asks me if I am sleeping or am I up for the day. Can we talk about what he want's to say? We met on the road and he told me that he does not want to meet me on the road for love any more. He does not want to leave his son. He has not yet let me meet the baby, the one that we were to have adopted together, and the one that was to be our child. Now he tells me that I am an angry person and that I am cold and a hard person.

I find this hard to believe if I was considered a neighborhood mom to about seventeen kids all of whom not one were mine and they all loved me dearly. Besides all of my nieces and nephews that I have, and great nieces and nephews that I have that love me dearly. He has never been around all these kids with me so how could he say these things. He just wants to spend the holidays with his son and spend the first six months of his life with him and then thinks he can call me when he wants and I am just going to let him back in my life because he calls.

He tells me that even though I said "I did not want him to call me that he was going to call me anyway when he wanted to." Who does he think he is and why does he think he can call when ever he wants?

# CHAPTER 21

I TRULY WISH I could meet someone else that would never let me look at him again and would take my thoughts away from him. Tammy the new owner works at the D Q I went next door for a sandwich and it took about fifteen minutes, it only took actually 3 minutes that I was gone. Tammy called me up and said "she was watching me on the camera and I was gone for fifteen minutes. I could not have been gone for more than three minutes because the owner of the sandwich shop was the one that made my sandwich. I tried to stay with her for her grand opening so that she could make a lot of money and it was a flop.

She did not make a lot of money and it was not worth my being there. I was decorating cakes and as I was standing there on my feet all day my back was literally killing me. I thought that I was going to get sick to my stomach from the pain. She could not understand this as this caused a big problem between us. She wrote me up and wanted me to sign these papers. I told her that I was not going to sign these papers and that I thought that she would be better off taking her key to the store.

I thought that the papers were a bit ridiculous. She said "that because I would not sign them that I would not work out for her." Well let me tell you, I have worked there for twelve years and all those little faces that come into that store come in looking for me. When they do not see me there they are definitely not going to come back to see her.

They come in and tell me that they don't want to see her, that they come in to see me. I will be around the shopping center working in another store. The owners of the other stores say that she was ridiculous to let me go because, I was such an asset to her store and that once the customers start to realize that I am not there they will not be coming back to her store. They will be going to another store and will be anxious to find out where I am. I will be next door at the other store that I worked at part time so they will see them there.

Today is Christmas Eve and she has to work the store by herself as she has nobody to work it. This is because she only has three employees. She wants to work them to no end. She wants to put additional duties on you and not give you additional pay. Yet she will give a part timer additional money to come in and work for her to cover when someone is sick. This is not fair to full time employees that have to work at a lesser rate of pay.

I would make all the novelties, make the cakes, clean all the fudge pumps, stock the store, run and make sure that the store had enough bread for the hot dogs and barbeque sandwiches, then came the time for the toilet tissue and paper towels to make sure that there was enough of this in the store. I was always cautious of these things and made sure that she had enough of these things in the store. This is all okay because she will have to do this all by herself and it won't be kept up. I truly feel sorry for the kids that are working for now as they are going to have a hard time working there.

I have been offered a management position in another restaurant. I told them that I would take the job and we will be discussing this matter after Christmas. It truly is her loss and their gain. Today we are doing a beautification of Christmas in the neighborhood. This is where all the houses put candles out at the end of the street in a waxed paper bag and light them at the end of the street at a certain time at night. I have not seen this so this will be my first time.

I wonder how my friend's husband is handling things. He never calls me anymore. This is the second year without his wife and son. I miss her and their son and I am sure it must be hard on him but when I call him he never answers the phone. It was okay to sit with him the first year and help him through the first Christmas, but it should be okay to also handle talking to your friends through out the rest of the time.

In the New Year I hope that a lot of things will change for all of us. I would like to meet someone new and just move on with my life and try to get things back in order. I wanted to open a restaurant and I have been approved for the funding for such a thing, I just might buy one here or take over an existing restaurant then see if I can make it work out. I was going to open a new one in another state however it would really get to Bob if I purchased the one that I might be thinking of buying. Not that it is any of his business, it just happens to be the one that he opened many years ago.

I think after Christmas I might go over and talk to him and just feel him out about the situation to see if he is interested in letting the restaurant go. If he is and is serious about the situation, then I will contact the people that I was talking to for the funding and see if I can get it for this state instead of leaving to another state. This way I won't have to worry about setting up a new one maybe in a year or so I could open a new one in another state, and have someone just run this one that I might trust to manage it. If it makes the money that it should be making I could pay off the loan and get another one started in another state.

I think that maybe this might be a good thing to do. He does not know that I am interested in buying his restaurant yet. I was going to go over and talk to him about getting started in another state and I asked the current employees not to say anything to him about me coming in to talk to him. I know that there is one waitress in particular that I do not care for there, and if I purchase the place I am sure that she would not stay. I would not necessarily ask her to leave but I am sure she would not feel comfortable working for me. When I come in I will not have her wait on me, as she is not very nice to me. This is why I am sure that she would not necessarily want to stay if I were to purchase this restaurant.

I occasionally run into some of the people that I worked with at the station and we talk about them being retired. One of them was hurt and he is not out on a disability. He is a very nice person. He could not get along with one of the commanders and after getting hurt he thought that it was better to just retire. The other one just retired because of the amount of time that he was on the department and felt that it was time to get out.

I have now gone to the cardiologist and they have said that "I will not have to have any surgery at this stage in my life which is very good. They think that if they change my medicine this could possibly help me and that I will have to go back to the cardiologist in two months and see." If this does not help then we will have to change our course of action. It is a good thing that there is no surgery to be done.

Time is just flying by. I am truly sorry that I sold my house to be with Bob and that I thought we would be together and raise a family as I probably should have known better than that. He thinks that I am still working at the D Q so when he thinks that he can call me there and I do not answer him he will get quite a bit a shock. If I can keep strong and not answer my phone to him, he will not know where I am because he does not have any other phone numbers for me.

This beautification night went off very nice in the neighborhood this evening. Everybody put out all of the candles and lighted them up at seven o'clock in the evening. All the homes in the neighborhood are decorated beautiful and the candles make them even more beautiful.

I will be with my three sisters and nieces and nephews and great nieces and nephews. This should be a lot of fun as they range from ten years old to one and a half. The one and a half years olds are twins. They are so funny. My brother in law dressed up as Santa Claus and my sister as an elf and the twins would not go near them. They cried so hard that no one could calm them down.

Then all of a sudden it became a curious thing to them that this big man in a red suit with a white beard was here and this little person in a red and green outfit was with him that some what sounded familiar. They just could not figure it out and then they had this curious look on there face but not daring enough to go over to Santa Claus. They wanted to stay with either mom or dad or an aunt that they were comfortable with. Then they started warming up when Santa was leaving.

Then came time to open the presents and there were so many of course they did not know what to play with first. They got these building blocks and that seemed to be the favorite one this evening. Sometimes the littlest ones are the best toys to give and they get the most enjoyment out of them. When it came time to go home they had to get some medicine and this did not go over very well with the boy. The girl took hers very well, but the boy was difficult. They tried to play the game that it was candy and that it tasted great and everybody was going to take some but he wasn't having any part of this. Then it had to be given the hard way. He was looking for someone that didn't participate in giving the medicine to him for that person to hold him, comfort him because he felt a little betrayed at this point. His whole day had been shattered at that point because he had been forced to take this medicine that he did not want to take.

Of course the clean up was done in an orderly manner. Everybody just pitched in and started doing the clean up. This just makes it a lot easier. It truly is hard to believe that it was Christmas Day and in one week it will be New Years Eve. Let's hope next year will be a great one and that things will change for the better. I would like to be in a different place and not be in the situation that I am in with my life. It would be wonderful to just start over somewhere else and leave all this behind as there is nothing here to hold me back.

My sister told me to take the extra food to the homeless people. My other sister asked "how would I know where they are located?" She said "where do you think she stayed when she didn't have a place to stay?" She said what did you mean? I said "when I was living on the highway, where did you think I was living when I didn't have a house to go to?" I guess you just don't get it.

It would be nice to just go to another state and leave this one just to purchase a new home and start a new life. Not to know anyone around and start new roots with a new job and meet new friends. This would be a change and maybe the best thing as a change would give a boost to your vitality.

I know that when I went to Europe I wanted to move to the Swiss Alps because I loved the atmosphere and it was so beautiful. It was not too cold and not too hot. I could get used to this climate and be comfortable there very easy. I don't think I would like the islands because it is too hot and muggy. I visited them once and I did not like them. I currently live in a hot atmosphere and I am not too impressed with the muggy and hot temperatures.

I am a person that likes the different changes of the seasons. I like to see the fall and see the leaves on the trees turn the colors to yellow, red, and then green. If you have never seen this you are truly missing a beautiful sight. I will take the rest of Christmas dinner that was left over which is truly a lot to the homeless and they can have a dinner that is cooked and have a decent one. There is no reason to throw it out when someone can eat. I will make sure that someone can have it because I will take it to the homeless shelter.

When I did not have a place to live and I had to live on the highway, I know that these people did not have any food so if I have to I will take it over to them and give it to them so they can have something to eat. I called the Fire Department to see if they wanted a Christmas dinner and if I could deliver it to them and they said "that they were delivered a dinner already but that they would check to see if there was a family around that either needed a dinner or would like a dinner delivered to them."

If something ever happened to me and I was in the area I would not have to worry about anything as nothing would happen to me because I made quite a few friends in that neighborhood. You have to make friends or you can be in a lot of trouble. It never hurts to be nice to people it will always come back to you in the end.

Well the Fire Department called back and we're not successful in getting anyone that wanted the dinner however, there is one other way that I think that I might be able to give this dinner away to. I usually give dinner or ice cream or something, I think I will bring it to the pharmacy that I always go to and they can have Christmas dinner for the midnight shift. There is enough for the whole store employees so that won't matter how many get some to eat.

To the fairytale end of the relationship that Bob and I had, I really hope that he gets the message and that he does not call me anymore. When he told me "that he did not want to deal with my family and that I was too cold and not soft, he really does not know me at all after all these years." After losing my house and having to move from place to place and some of the things that you do for this, well you have to bide your time and keep on going. It's not easy and I know it's not my house so I have to abide by the rules however some of them are a little hard. This does not make me want to speak to him ever again after looking back and knowing what I have lost and worked so hard for.

Well a New Year is coming up and maybe it will bring new and better things. I tried to get a hold of the people in charge of the restaurant deal today and there was no answer. I will try them again tomorrow. I certainly do not want to loose my deposit if I can help it. When I last spoke to the gentleman he told me that I could possibly get my deposit back because I was having heart trouble and that I would have to speak to a certain person. However, when I tried to call him today, he did not answer the phone. I left him a message and I have not received a phone call back. I will call again tomorrow.

I was so excited about starting the restaurant and I was going to have my niece go ahead and work with me. She was as excited as I was but now that I am having medical problems and cannot do this at this time, she understands and I am having trouble getting a hold of these people. I will continue to call them until I can reach them. I do not feel this is fair and I realize that it is the holidays but I do at least expect a return phone call.

My restaurant would have been called Wings and Curls of the city I was going to move to and then have everybody come to my grand opening. They were as excited as I was about the program and we were all working so hard until I got sick. The program was placed on hold and when I called and spoke to the gentleman he told me that he would do everything in his power to get my deposit back to me. Yet when I talked to the other gentleman, he was to email me a letter and I have not received it as of this date. I called again today and there is no answer.

I hope that they are not just playing games with me and that I can truly get my deposit back as this will truly make me sick to my stomach if I lost this amount of money. It is nothing to sneeze about. I will however continue to save as much as I can and put it in my savings account until I find out what will happen. A hard lesson to learn and one well learned in a short amount of time.

As I walked by the Dairy Queen to get something from the grocery store today, my old boss came out and called me. She said to me "Lee-Ann, here is your mail and Tammy needs your forwarding address for your mail." I told her "don't worry about it as I have already taken care of it. I transferred my mail to another mail facility so she won't have to worry about it." I asked her "How was your Christmas, I hope it was good?" She said "it was good for the kid's, and peaceful for me that am all I really wanted." I said "that's nice, I am truly glad that you had a nice Christmas. I hope to see you around." She said "me too." I said "you will. Don't worry. I'm not going anywhere."

My customers are already asking where I am and when will I be back? When they tell them that I am not there any longer the customers make the comment that they will no longer come back to the store because I am not there. They will find somewhere else to get there ice cream. I have only been gone for a week. That is pretty sad. I was at this store for twelve years. She is truly going to suffer for the decision to let me go.

I truly wish I had my own home at this point and did not sell it because of Bob. When I think of it I get a little hot under the collar, because I could have done things a lot different if I did not sell my house when I did. Today I learned that my niece got engaged, the one that I go and see that lives in Georgia. That is truly exciting. My brother-in-law's wallet is going to start smoking like a gun. That will be a big wedding.

Would you have to wonder if it feels that you have a friend in a friend when you call your friend to get together and spend a little time with her and you have been friends for thirty years and she says "she will call you back, this is about four hours ago, and she has not called you yet." Sometimes you let it go and you don't call her for days and you get involved in what you need to do and when she calls you act like nothing ever happened and then she will call and say that she got tied up.

Yet when she wants to get together you are there for her and you are not tied up. Must you always be available for everybody or is it okay to sometimes say that you are busy when you are not just to let them know how it feels the way you are treated? I truly wonder sometimes if I packed my bags and moved somewhere else and started over where no-one knew me would things be different for me because I would make new friends and then I would not have these feelings of being on the outside all the time. They are the hardest to deal with especially at the holidays.

This is why I wanted to go and start my restaurant in another city from where I live now. With my health the way it is, I am not sure I can do this until I get it straight. For the mean time I must do what the doctors say and try not to stress myself out.

I truly know this man and I would not put it past him that after the New Year that he does try and contact me and say "that he is sorry and that he wants to get a hold of me and that he wants to get back together because he misses me and that for all the years that we have been together that it was a mistake to break up and we should be together and we were made for each other."

However I have been doing some soul searching and after all the things that he has said to me this time I think that I would prefer to just meet someone else and go on with my life. I know that when one door closes another one will open if you let it. So I need to let this close and move on. No matter how much time and effort I have put into the relationship and no matter how much I loved this man I truly need to leave it alone and look forward.

Besides he is the one that said "he did not want to deal with my family, that I take too much medicine, and that he did not want to feel like he was ninety years old." So after being in a relationship with someone for so long as we have been and hearing this would you have anything to say to him? I truly do not think so. When he asked me if I had anything to say, I said "NO." What was there to say? You said it all. I was just waiting to hear his excuse on the phone not even a phone call this morning. He could not even tell me this face to face.

Well today I worked with the young man that I truly like working with and I don't have to ask this youngster to do much of anything. He said to me "I really don't feel good and don't feel like dealing with the customers today so if you don't mind, I will scrub the floors today because they need it." I said "I don't mind if I get in a bind then I will have you help me." He said "okay, fair enough." Well everything went okay and the floors look great. He finished just before we were to close and I let the owner know what he did so that they could appreciate the job. They love this kid as much as I do and he is such a great person to work with. The owners gave only some of us Christmas bonus's this year so we did not say anything to the other employees as of course this could cause a problem.

We had one employee that was to come to work just before going on vacation and she did not check to see if she was scheduled so when I called her to see if she was coming in she said "I was not to be on the schedule until after the 22$^{nd}$ of December as I was on vacation until then." Well I wound up pulling a double that day as I do this quite often. I am used to doing this in the restaurant business. She is scheduled to be on the schedule as of the 28$^{th}$ but I don't know if she will be in or not so I am planning to work a double again tomorrow just in case she does not show.

It is the holidays and you never know if she might not get home in time or if the traffic on the road will permit. So I told the owner that I would work if she does not show. Besides I am an adult and they are kids so if they want to go and have fun it is okay. I don't go out and drink so I am not worried about going to a lot of parties. With all the drunks on the road I would rather be at home or at work anyways. It is safer to be there than on the road. After being the victim of three car accidents I would not want to be the victim of another one as these have been enough.

Today is Thursday and I have been at work all day. I worked a double and I got a phone call from the company that I was dealing with for the loan for the restaurant that I wanted to start up. They sent me a letter to sign that releases me of any responsibilities from them and any responsibilities of them from me so that I can get my deposit back. This is good news for me as I was truly afraid I was not going to get my money back. I told the gentleman that as I was driving down the road the other day I started having chest pains and as I called the doctors office he told me to come into his office immediately. When I got there he put the EKG machine on me to make sure I was not having a heart attack and then he told me that we need the results of the other tests before we will know what is going on.

When I got home tonight I received a phone call from the kid at the Dairy Queen asking me how to get milk to make shakes. I truly wanted to tell him to call his owner, that I do not work for them any more and that it is her job to tell him. Being that I am not a bitch to the kids, I told him what to do and he was truly appreciative for my help.

He told me that he had to cover for one kid because she had to leave and there was no one else to cover. This would not have happened if I were still there as it would have been my night to work. He also told me that he lost a sale of four shakes because he did not have any milk to make shakes. This is the owners fault as she should make sure that there are enough supplies on hand for all shifts. When I worked there these supplies were always on hand.

If you want to get mad at me because I should not be on ladders when I have no business on them, and because I could not finish a cake then that is your problem. However if you supposedly went to school to learn to do cakes, then you could have finished the cake in five minutes. I told her that if I had to finish the cake that particular night it would have looked like it and I'm sure you can understand that. If you have ever seen a cake that looks like someone should not have been decorating the cake on a particular day it will show up in the decorations. She could have done it in a short amount of time.

Instead she wanted to be a fool and write me up and expected me to sign these papers which I was not going to do so I told her that I was leaving and to have a nice day. I see some of my customers in the grocery store and they say "I will see you at Dairy Queen." And I have to tell them no I'm sorry I don't work there any more." They ask why and I just say "I got a better job offer."

I don't bad mouth her as she is doing to me. She is going around telling everybody that she fired me. If she continues to do this then she will loose her business. It is not the same as it was. She does not make the same amount as it did when I worked there. She asked the old owner if "she would decorate her cakes, and I don't know if she is or not but she better learn how to do this."

# CHAPTER 22

I can not believe that New Years is only two days away. It does not seem possible. This year has just flown by. I hope that I can get everything together and get my own place where I can get things settled where I want them and not have to have everything in different places. And that I can close the storage facility and save that money.

As the elections went on this year, there were quite a few judges that ran that asked if they could place the posters in the window of the ice cream shop? When the one owner had the store she let one in particular place the poster in the window. Her secretary told me that she would help me in writing my book. Well shortly after the elections and needless to say I have not been able to get a hold of her. I will continue to write this myself and without her assistance.

Today is Saturday and I was visiting old friends around the Dairy Queen, when Tammy came out and asked my friend at sub way "if he would change the register tape for her in her store because she did not know how. " He said "No because of the things that she did to me he would not help her in any way. He wants nothing to do with her and the store."

I was then visiting some friends down at another store called Rookies when she came into the store and the one kid named Big-Don said "awkward" and when we looked up she came into the store and was looking for the owner of the store to see if he would come down to the Dairy Queen and change the register tape for her because she could not do this her self. All she would have had to do is to ask me and I might have done it for her or showed her if she was decent about it, but being that she wants to act like an idiot I will not do anything for her or help her in any way.

This is not my store and I do not have to be nice and show her anything as she should be able to figure it out by herself. I told her how to do this several times and she still cannot get this information. Her daughter was with her today and she waved to me and I waved back at her. There is no animosity us it is just her mother.

I wanted to speak with the girl that was working today for a little while as she paged me the other day and I just wanted to make sure that she did not need me for anything personal. She said "it was not personal it was for the store and she did not think that I would have returned the call if I were called from the store number." I told her "she was right, that if she called me from the store I would not have returned the call because I do not work there and I don't see the need to return the calls." When I went into talk to her today, the store was not stocked properly and the fudge pumps were dirty, fudge was coming out of the side of the pumps.

This is not supposed to be like this and they can get written up for this as it means that the pumps have not been cleaned in a long time. I know this and if I were to call on this she could get in a lot of trouble. I can get the number to the district manager and get her in a lot of trouble or just write Dairy Queen a letter.

If I wanted to be a mean person I could do these kinds of things however that are not my style. When her district manager comes in and sees that things are not being cleaned as they should be and not being stocked as they should be, she can be told to close the doors. The young lady told me that "she got a better job offer and she was not sure that she was going to stay there because she felt that she was doing all the work." I told her "that I felt that way as well when I worked there because nobody ever did anything and that she paid someone else more money to come in and cover me when I had the flu for three days while I was out and would not give me a raise.

Yet the more you do the more she will put on you to do and she will not give you a raise. " This is not correct and I have been there for a long time. You just don't treat your employees that way. It truly is funny that she would not say anything to me. Everybody around there feels uncomfortable around her when she shows up and I am there talking to them regardless as to the subject. It could be the weather or something personal and they feel uncomfortable if she comes in and I might be there, even after all these years. This is not right.

Today is New Years Eve and I stopped to have breakfast at my favorite restaurant. I saw a few of my usual customers and they asked me why I was not at the Dairy Queen. I sat and talked with them for a while and when they found out the truth, they could not believe it as they have known me for several years. They said to me "that I shall go on to bigger and better things in life and not to worry about what she thinks because it will be her loss." We talked for a while and then I told them I had to go and to have a wonderful New Years and a safe one. I went over to wish my co-workers at subway a safe and wonderful New Years, and see if they needed anything while I was in the neighborhood.

I got them some change that they needed and we talked for a while then I left. I have to work for a while today and then I am not sure what I will do to ring the New Year. I have to work tomorrow morning like everyone else and I don't like being on the road with all the drunk drivers. I hope that it is busy at work today, that way it won't linger on. I must get ready for work now.

Today I was talking to a gentleman about a movie I saw last night. His reaction to the movie was very interesting to me. When I described the movie, he said to me "that seems to be the American way." As I thought about it and as I look at what Bob did in out relationship and never committing to me, yet committing to others and just thinking that he can do whatever he darn well pleases, he thinks this does not bother anyone, I wonder if there are any other men out there that do not treat women like this or are they all the same? Do they think that women are just out to hurt them? Can't we all just act like were suppose to and be in relationships and act friendly towards each other? I would just like to meet someone that I could have a life with and move on. I guess if its in the cards I will and then he will have to go away.

My boss at subway called me today and told me that he was going to place me in another store as a manager and teach me all the paperwork. This will enable me to do both stores that I work at and I will have about six to ten kids under me. All the kids that currently work with me now we get along just fine so that would be no problem. I know all the customers at the store next to the Dairy Queen so they will come in looking for me there as they already are and I will just serve them subs instead of ice cream.

That's not a problem, being that the witch did what she did. It really doesn't matter to me after all money is money no matter where it comes from. I tried to call one of my girlfriends to wish her a Happy New Year and she would not pick up the phone. I wonder what that was all about My other girlfriend is working and has not returned my call since the other day. I understand when you get a little busy, but when you act like you never have time for your friend's well that's a different story. When you really need them don't think that they will be there for you because they don't always forget the hurt that is caused no matter what it is.

I truly promise myself that the next house that I get no matter where it is I will not loose it for anybody. When your so called friends don't call you back then it is time to change them also.

I guess it's time to go back to the cardiologist as I am having chest pains as I am driving down the street. I am also having them when I am walking. I must go to the primary doctor and find out what the other test results were and bring them to the cardiologist as he needs this information. It would probably help him in his decision in what would be the correct course of action as to the treatment that is best for me. When these pains strike they do not tickle. I am scheduled to have an appointment in February however I do not think it is the best thing to do to wait until my appointment, so maybe I should call the office and let the doctor know what is going on and let him decide what to do.

I have been offered a managers position in a other restaurant and it would be that I will work in two different restaurants and manage them while working with the kids and training them correctly, and I would teach my current kids to do more paper work if they wanted to know more and then teach them the management side of the restaurant. I have one kid who works with me that takes control in starting a project that needs to be done without being told to do it and finishes it without asking for help before the store will close. He will not let me do the floors or take the trash out or do any heavy work of any sort. We work hand in hand and it goes so easy and so fast that the night goes by and before you know it, it is over. He's such a good kid and I love working with him.

The owners think of me as part of the family and when I called them with the totals they sometimes hand the phone over to their son so that he can say "hello" and I ask him "How are you? Are you okay? What are you doing?" He would say something like I was playing football today, and that I was having fun." I told him to have fun and be careful because I would not want anything to happen to my sweetheart. I love you. He said "Okay. I will see you later." I will be fine at Subway and be a manager there.

Now what is different is that Bob thinks he is all of everything in that of telling me that he did not want to meet me on the road for love any more. He did not want to put up with my family and that his not even one year old son has a positive attitude and that I am negative and cold and hard, that he does not want to see me.

When he thinks that he can call me anytime he wants to and I am suppose to answer his beck and call, he has another thing coming much to his surprise. This time he has gone too far. He called me and told me that "he could not find his tag information and wanted to know what to do in order to get his tags." I told him to contact Tallahassee.

If we were still together I would have just told him to send me the information I would have needed to go down to the tag agency and get him his new tags and sent them to him. But if we are over I don't see the need to be so helpful to him. Let him learn how to do things for himself. And if I am so cold and hard let him see just how cold and hard I truly can be. This will truly be an eye opener for him as he does not know that I can play being a bitch like anybody else. I helped him in the past as he could not get things straighten out but I am not going to do this now. He is a big boy and a daddy now he will have to figure it out by himself.

I was talking to a friend of mine today about him and he said "I am surprised that you would even give him that much information as to finding out where to get the tags. I am sure he could find this out by himself. If not well someone else would have to do this for him. Don't fall into his trap again.

He will probably call you and say "Oh honey could you help me because I have the baby and I can't get my tags done and the christening is coming up and I don't have time to do the research on the tags, could you do me a favor and get them for me?" Then I will just have to say "well I guess not because I am not your honey and I am not allowed to pick them up for you anymore as we are not an item any longer." I know him and when he gets back from vacation and in the office he will be calling me this week. I will be very busy and not able to answer the phone call or just have to miss it.

Then he will get the surprise of his life when he calls Dairy Queen looking for me and I am no longer there. Because I did not call him and tell him that I left. He will call and say "why didn't you call and tell me that you are not working at Dairy Queen? When did you quit Dairy Queen? What happened to make you leave? I bet you are much happier now that you left, aren't you? Come on you got to admit you were beginning to hate it there any way." These will be the things that will come out of his mouth.

I contacted the company again about the money for the restaurant that I was going to open today, and they told me that I could not recuperate the money, however I could have the services of the business for six months if I got better. The most they could do is to extend the services for six months after that if I still wasn't any better they would take it from there. The owners at Subway, I am sure will be upset if I purchased it but I am sure that they can understand, however I could purchase it and let the managers that are running it do their jobs and leave it the way it is. I could just come to do the books and scheduling and check out everything. I know that the store is running fine with the staff that is there. I would have to talk to some of them and see if this would be okay with them if they would want to stay on as managers and I would only be around in the background.

I have a friend that wanted to get into the restaurant business and I have not talked to her about this yet, I could talk to her and see how she feels. As this is not and ice cream stores it is a full sit down dinner place just a finger eating type place. It does not require that you eat with silverware on every plate that is served. That is the difference. The other girl that I was going to start the restaurant with me backed out and now she will not even return my calls. I tried to call her and wish her a happy New Year and she won't even pick up the phone. I really don't think that is very nice. That is why I have reservations about asking my other friend if she is interested in going into the business with me.

If I do this it will be strictly by myself. This young man that I work with, tells me tonight that he wants to clean the ice machine. I don't have to ask him to do anything. This is the kind of employee that you wish you had all the time.

I went over to the restaurant and inquired weather or not he would be interested in selling it and the manager told me that after he had his stints placed in his heart he wanted to keep it for a couple of more years before getting rid of the restaurant. Then I asked her if he would maybe help me with some of the background information as so that would make it easier to open one in another state and she said I would have to talk to him and let him make that decision for himself. If I am going to open one in a different state what difference would it make if I needed to ask some questions from him about the operations of the kitchen? Some people feel threatened by others wanting to get ahead in life and that's just wrong. I know that if I was approached and someone asked me do to this and they wanted to open one in an other state why not let them? It truly comes back to you in many ways.

I hope this year will be a better one but as the saying goes it will only be what you make of it. Let the past be the past and future be the future. I must go for now but I shall be back.

# CHAPTER 23

TODAY IS THURSDAY AND I received a phone call from Bob. He said "he could not believe that he could not get a hold of the company that I invested my money with and he was the agent. He had such a hard time with the company before he went on vacation in December. He was going to make some more phone calls tomorrow and then he was going to call me back and let me know the out come." I told him "that at this point he could cancel the investments with the company and get a check for the amount of the investments that I have which are large sums of money and bring the money to me. That I can not afford to loose any more money at this point in my life.

I would put it some place a little safer than the investment of his company and that I did not have much faith in his company at this point." He then asked me to meet him in the beginning of February and I asked him "why?" He said "he wanted to meet with me" He did not explain himself as to why. If he thinks it is going to be just as the relationship was before he has another thing coming. Not after what he had to say to me just last month, give me a break I do not turn my emotions on and off like a light switch.

What happened to I was hard, cold, and I was not soft. I was not positive and he did not want that around his son. Did his vacation not go the way he wanted it to. Maybe he is out of money and he needs me to bring him some, as I bet you that is what he is going to tell me that I have to visit with his buddy to have him go to his mom's house and then go to his place and pick up the envelope and bring it to him.

Then I am supposed to have the weekend with him and everything is supposed to be okay.

However this times after all the hard words there was no apology from him or flowers sent to apologize for his actions just a call asking if I would meet him to talk. You would think that he would try and find out if his buddy would get a hold of me and send me some flowers on his behalf and do a little more to try and get me back than just a phone call. I am quite pissed off at him for what he said and his actions and I do need to meet with him only to get the money from his company. However I can get the money sent to me by Fed Ex.

The only reason I would go is to find out what he wants and to see if he is just trying to use me. I know that he doesn't know a lot of things and he is hinting around to see if I will say okay, I will help you do this and that. He has called and said that he is getting the run around about his tags because he lost the information in moving and it truly is very simple to get, but I am not going to offer to do this after the way he treated me and I am not his girlfriend at this time. He made himself quite clear as to what he wanted and I am not an associate to anyone. He has a lesson to learn about how to treat someone and I will teach him how it feels to be treated like this.

He called me again and said "that he was in training and after he got out of training he would call the office and see if he could find out any information on my investments. I have not heard from him today so I do not think that he called today. He will probably call on Monday." I will be busy at work as my boss will be out of town and if any of the kids do not show then I will have pull there shifts.

That is just part of being a manager. He will not be back until Monday. That's okay I can always use the extra money. I went to go to one of my favorite restaurant's today and when I got there today it was closed up. The building was being torn down. That is a shame as I have been going there for thirty years. It is a little Chinese place and it is a little whole in the wall. It has the best food around. I wonder if they got bought out by some big building plaza. I wonder if they are going to move to another place. I will have to call the number and see if they answer it and maybe find out if they moved to a different location, that's an idea. My friend an I went out to eat today and we were going to go there that is how we found out that it was closed. Instead we wound up going to a steak house and she did not enjoy her dinner very well. My dinner was very good.

I stopped in to talk to my kids at the Dairy Queen and my girl that used to work for me told me that she cut her hours down to two days so that she could study for school because she was not going to fail this semester. The store was dirty and not stocked. She said "that she is tired of being the only one that stocks the store and not getting any help." As I was sitting there waiting for her she had some customers come in and inquire about the cakes, and she could not answer there questions.

I told them the answers they wanted to know and they were very great full for that. They purchased a cake and then another customer came in looking to purchase a cake. She had to change the bags of milk in the refrigerator so she was not directly behind the counter, so the customer could not get the answer they wanted right away and they left. I do not work there any more so I did not feel that it was my responsibility to answer any body's questions. I was nice enough to help out my girl but I did not have to that. I will not go out of my way to help the owner from what she did to me.

If the kids need me and I a there I might go ahead and help them, but I will not go out of my way to assist her. Then the second one comes in and says "that he is training a kid and he better not have an attitude because he was not in the mood for one tonight." I don't know this kid but that is no way to start with him. The owner should have been with him or had him train with a more experienced person not the one that was there tonight, but this is not my business. This store is going to go down hill real fast. The sales will disappear and the customers will not come back. Lets see how long she will last. The other store owners say not longer than maybe six months.

I went to a little Italian restaurant called Imari's today and applied for a position as a part time waitress. I needed to do something as the money that I made before is not coming in and it needs to be replaced.

I can not get back the investment that I put in for the one that I was going to start up so I need to start saving this back again. The only way to do this is to get another job and place all of the money that I make from it into a savings account. I am still not sure if I want to meet Bob after what he had to say to me.

He was pretty hard on me and I am truly mad at him. That just seems like I would be going back for more. My room-mate wants to raise my rent and I truly don't think that it is worth the raise. I don't really cook there. I may wash a couple of shirts with hers and watch the news but other than that I am not home. She quit all the jobs she had so she thinks that she needs to raise my rent so that all her money can be re-cooperated and if she thinks that it will settle with me, she needs to think again because with all the restrictions that she likes to put on people well I won't stay there very long.

I would like to move away and just get a fresh start somewhere else, in a different state and a different change of scenery. I have had to loose my pet and all of my furniture and now I need to go through my storage shed to see what I can get rid of and what I need to keep as I am just storing it for no reason at this moment and if I could put it in a yard sale then I am sure that I could sell it for and make a profit off it instead of it just sitting there doing nothing. When I finally get my house I can always purchase new dishes and things that I might need. At least this way I wouldn't have to pay a storage shed bill every month.

Today is Bob's birthday and I have not even called him to wish him a Happy Birthday, which is not like me because that is something I always did. I am torn apart about what he said just before Christmas and whether or not I want to call and wish him greetings on his birthday. I still don't know if I want to meet him or not next month in Savannah , GA. He truly hurt me this time and after all we have been through and what he made me loose, I truly am having a hard time forgiving him for what has been said and done.

Well I am scheduled to work at two different stores tonight and I must get a hold of the owner and find out what he wants me to do. That is strange as this does not happen to often. I spoke to the owner and

I will be at the one store and the other kid will be at the other store. My young lady that worked for me at Dairy Queen is very fed up with the owner and is ready to walk out. She told me this evening that she thinks that the owner is selling the store because everything is out of stock again and this is a sign that the store is going to be sold. I can not blame her when no body else does anything and you are the only one that does it all, it gets very annoying. She would be very likely to come to Subway if allowed.

That was my beef with her and that is why I left. My other boss said "tell her to walk out he would take her in a heart beat, I told her that I want to talk to her so when she gets a chance to come out side so we can talk. I will check on her in a minute to see if she is busy. I went over and told her that if she wanted to leave that my boss told me that he said he would hire her if she wanted to leave." She said "Okay. She was not giving her a hard time. It's just that the store is not stocked and that nobody does anything." They are not busy like they used to be at all.

My boss brought his wife and son in to see me today. They are so lovely. One of my customers came into the Subway and asked me why I do not work next door anymore? I said "I got a better offer. If there was a different owner maybe I would go back and work there in the morning and on my days off here. Not presently with the owner it has." She just looked at me and said "I understand. That's a darn shame you have been there so long and we all thought you owned the place." I said "I didn't own it." She said "you worked it like you owned it and that's what made the difference.

It showed and you always took care of everything as if it was your own." I said "you should so that it doesn't get broken and things get respected that way. It doesn't matter who's they are." She just shook her head and said "your right." My rescue friends came by today to check up on me and see if I was okay. Even though I work next door they still want to make sure that I am okay. When I worked at the Dairy Queen they wanted to know if I was okay from having chest pains and what the status of my last doctor's appointment was. They picked me up five times in one year so I really appreciate them coming in just to check up on me and see if I was okay. They are so nice and I really wouldn't mind going out with one of them. There are quite a few nice guys that are not married and are good looking.

I would like to talk to the kids tonight but it is a little to late and I can not talk to them on the internet as I can not get on it from where I am at. I will have to write them a letter and ask them to send me the pictures to my email address instead of the photo shop that they send it to as I am having trouble getting the pictures of the baby from there. My great niece is so adorable and I have only seen her in pictures but you never know I just might surprise the kids and go and see them in person one day. I think I will call up Bob and ask him "why he wants to meet me, because I just have to know from the last conversation that we had, I had nothing to say to him and if he was so cold and hard to me why he would want to be with me?

I wouldn't think it was just for sex, because he truly could get that any where he wanted to. He's not a bad looking man and now he's free because his divorce is final. What is so special about meeting with me? Besides I need to know if he found out anything on my investments.

If the owner of the Dairy Queen is selling the store, then when the New owners come in they would have a hard time unless the kids tell them that I worked there and now I work next door if they needed me they could get a hold of me and if the owner came over and introduced themselves to me maybe I would be interested in coming over and helping them, as it is now with the present one, no way. My interview at the Italian restaurant went very well and I think I will have a good chance at getting a couple of days a week to get back on my feet. If I can get a Saturday night and maybe a Tuesday night and even a Wednesday day this would be very helpful. If he asked me to work more weekday days then I would, I just have to keep Monday and Friday days off which I already told him.

He is aware of this and said "he would work with my situation and see what he could do." I will ask the man above to help me and if it is in his power then I shall get the job part time." I need to go to sleep and I am doing a double tomorrow.

It is really funny my girlfriend thinks that she has the upper hand on me for the inter-net but little does she know that I can go to Kink's and look things up there and have no problems. This is what I am doing and without any problems from her. This is awfully nice wouldn't you think. My little buddy that used to work at Subway is now going into the Navy, now that is a total switch. Wonders never seize to amaze you.

# CHAPTER 24

I AM WORKING AT the main Subway and trying to bring up the sales. There is another office building going up and I will try and bring these people in with coupons to our Subway. Maybe try some buy one get one free. Or with the current two for $8.99 specials that are going on coupons. Whatever it takes to get them back in the store, then again school starts tomorrow so this will also help and on Saturday mornings if I worked it here with the kids I could pick up the sales if the kids knew that I was here. I would push the sales and pizza sales.

Making them specials and combination specials for lunch, my boss wants me to go by and offer them 10% off on Saturday mornings because these kids know me but I would have to work the counter because the kids won't have it any other way. This is something he needs to understand. These kids don't want anyone else working with them, just like when I was doing these kinds of specials Dairy Queen. If I did this with Subway they would bring in so much business that it would be unreal.

I spoke to my manager about doing this a he totally agrees with me as it would bring in the kids on Saturday mornings. If I can work with my girlfriend on Saturday mornings we could really kick butt because we work well together as a team. If we needed her son we would get him to help us as well. This would make it all worth while because I would get some cards from the guy that owns the hobby shop down the way and use it to my advantage like I did at D. Q.

I would not charge the kids extra for the meals to buy the cards, I would say "try your luck at a Yugi Oh card and see if you can get a good one and use about four or five cards that do not mean anything in with the meals to get the kids back into the store. This is what I did at DQ and it worked so well that I literally sold so many hot dog lunches on Saturday mornings that it was unbelievable.

The new owner now charges the kids extra money for the cards and it is too much money so the kids do not want to purchase the meals from her. If they know that I am there on Sat. and that I am working the meals the way I did at DQ I know that they will be there for the meal deals. Besides I used to let them come in and play the card games at the table all day. This did not bother me, I would tell them that if a customer came in they had to offer the table up to the customer and if the customer did not want the table then I did not care if they stayed at the table.

However, they had to purchase something in order to use the table because it was for paying customers only. So if one of the kids at the table paid for something that was okay, then the rest could join him. Usually all of them purchased something though because they got hungry watching one of them eating something. Or they would buy Nachos because they would like the smell of them. Or an ice cream cone or a blizzard or some type of ice cream dish. But the kids always respected me and the rules of the store. If I ever needed anything, they were always there to help me, and I truly appreciated that, it didn't matter what it was.

It is still that way. The kids sit down and talk to me as if I were there older sister, or there Aunt. They have known me since they were little kids and are now teenagers. It is nice to have that respect from all these kids and they are not even yours. Yet the one that lives in the house that I live in just cannot get it in his head that I am not a bad person and if he would just straighten up and not expect that the world is at his beck and call, his world would be a lot easier.

He likes to play his parents too much because in his mind he wants them to get back together. He has been with his father for a month and has been peaceful around here. She goes and spends time with him and I can not be happy for her. She works in the day. Then comes home and gets him and has dinner with him then takes him back to his dad's house. That's okay with me even if he were here, as long as I do not have to baby sit him anymore. So I called him from my cell phone and he told me that he wanted to go to Pakistan and he wanted to teach me the paperwork at Subway so he was going to come in the morning to do this. He is from there and wants to take his family there for a visit. I think he is a little home sick for his culture. It is different here and he wants to take his wife and son back home. He has said this couple of times to me and he also said "that he was thinking of selling his stores and moving back to Pakistan." He hasn't told anyone else this information yet and he said "that he has enough money that he could live comfortably in Pakistan."

I hope he does not sell the stores because if he did I truly do not know if I would want to work for anyone else at the one store. The second store is okay, the manager there is fine. We get alone great. I work with him side by side and he is funny. We don't have any problems working together and he will tell me to leave a list of things for the night crew to do because if it is in his hand writing it might not get done as the kids respect me as the manager and him as the owner. They like me very much and love working with me.

They say that we work together and it works like butter. I will help them and do just as much as they do and not expect them to have to do all the work by themselves and just watch over them or sit on the phone all day I think that is why they respect me so much. The owner does not do this as well and that is why we along too. He does just as much as the next guy. He will not let me lift anything that is heavy as I am not aloud to do this. I will be on the floor for lifting heavy items.

I have customers that come in and will not let me lift a thing. If something is to heavy they will literally lift it for me because they know that I can not do it. They have seen that it will take the air right out of me and that I will be on the floor and I will have to call Fire Rescue.

I have a gentleman who comes in with his two boys. He lost his wife about six months ago due to natural causes. The boys took to me and we sit and read stories and play cards or talk and see how school is doing or just play around. When the little one would get ready to leave he would jump up in my arms and literally start kissing me for about fifteen minutes and not stop. We would go through this every time he came into the store and every body thought that they were my kids.

All the customers that were around used to think that it was the cutest thing when he would do this, if he were in the back of the line he would run to the front and come around the counter and jump into my arms because he loved me so much. This child took to me as a second mother, I did not mind and I don't think his father did either. What lovely boys he has. I still say, I'll see my boys later.

I had a lady come in and order party platters the other day, which was no problem. I started to work on them as they were due at 2:00 pm. I had to make two of them and they require about an hour of your time to make. She called and asked "if she could have a third party platter made and if she could pick it up at the same time?" I said "sure that it would be no problem." Well this takes an additional seven loafs of bread and three party platters takes twenty one loafs. It takes two hours to raise bread. I had to make extra bread and serve customers and then my computer would not start up so I had to call my other manager in and he had to come in and get the computer started so I could run the register. He asked "what I was doing?" I told him I had three party platters due at 2:00 pm." He said "do you need any help?" I said "if you would like to start my other bread for the day I would appreciate it as I am a little behind from trying to get the computer to start."

He started my breads and then just hung around with me for a while. He is such a nice guy. I have a wonderful team of managers. I love working with these guys. I can talk to them about anything. They will help me with whatever I need help with. The other one told me that he thinks of me as family as well today. That is a very high compliment from them.

I was at my girlfriend Lou's house today and we were talking about the restaurant that I was going to open. When I told her what happened and that I was starting to have chest pains and the doctor advised me to not get in an investment of this nature with this happening to me she suggested that I place the investment on EBay to sell and have her son and his friend place for me. She will call them tomorrow for me and ask them to do this as they have the knowledge, and they can sell this easy for me and I will not loose my investment or money.

This is a good thing because I can not afford to loose this much money that I had saved up. We had a bet that it would not take Bob long to call me and ask me to meet him and it only took him four days into the new year to call and say that he missed me and that I am suppose to go to his friend and obtain money from him. I thought that he sold his house and if he did why doesn't he have money? Is he just a bunch of more lies?

I would not know this unless I go and meet him and talk to him as he wants me to because he will not tell me anything on the phone. He never has and he is not about to start changing now. My girlfriend told me to come over and use the internet at her house and not to pay for it at some office business store, as this is ridiculous. We have been friends too long for something like that. If I needed some help with something the kids could probably help me anyway as they probably know more about computers than we do. Lets face it, unless you take a computer class these days and you are not in classes with them then the kids get them in there classes and they do know more than you. Unless you are a programmer or you build them.

Today is Thursday and I am working at US1 Subway. The phone is ringing and the other young lady asked me to answer it for her. I told her I would do so. When I picked up the phone I said "Good morning Subway may I help you?" The gentlemen on the line said "First of all may I say that I have called about three other subways and I did not get greeted that way on the phone. He then proceeded to say that he wanted to order three party platters and about fifty bags of chips and some sodas and asked me how much this would cost?"

I told him to give me his name and number and I would contact the owner and I would then call him right back with a price. The owner told me contact him and find out when he needed this and gave me a price of approximately $145.00. I called the gentleman back and told him that it would cost him this price and that he would be smarter to look in the sale papers for the soda because he could get it for four for $10.00 as he wanted assorted sodas and he wanted it in bottles or he could get it on sale in the grocery store between now and the time that he wanted the party platters." He told me "that he would put the information on the board and get back with me about the platters and would most likely be ordering them from our store and was very appreciative of the information that I gave him.

Then he told me to have a nice day and he would call me soon. I told him "to have a nice day and I hope to be doing business with him soon."

Today is Friday and we are at a different store and it started out slow. I went to get some breakfast before I started work and some fruit. We had the food truck coming today and I knew that we would not be able to get out so I went out and got it early. My old boss was having breakfast and she did not have too much to say. Just a few words, hi how are you, by just small talk. When I got back to the store we had a few customers and then I asked the other partner if we needed to do any prep work? He said "No as there would be two people at night. We had a few customers and I didn't think anything of it.

Then these gentlemen came in and all of sudden and he said "I have a big order can you handle it? I said "yes sir." He said "I need twenty four subs for a for a photo shoot for a commercial." He gave me a list of what he needed and then went to Publix and I started on them and he came back and I had them half finished and then he was labeling them as I finished them. I finished them and had other customers as well. I had no walk outs as well. Our food truck came in today as well in the middle of all of this. What a busy day we had. Then we slowed down and finished our prep work. I hope the night shift had a great day as well. I will have to talk to the young lady tomorrow.

This weekend will be a long one. It is a three day weekend and that will mean that there will be a lot of kids around the shopping center. I am planning on putting up a Saturday special for about three hours and see what I can do for the store. My girlfriend and I went into Dairy

Queen today and it was a mess. The young lady that was working it was sitting out side smoking a cigarette and then got up and serviced customers without washing her hands. The store is not stocked. They have a rookie serving customers without someone in the store at all times to make sure that there are no mistakes to the products. The walls are dirty and the ice cream freezers are filthy. The store was not run this way when I was working or managing it.

It truly needs to have an inspector walk into the store without being given a heads up that he will be there, because it is sad that the store is being run down like this. The new owner now has to go to ready made cakes because she cannot get anyone to make them, as she burned the bridge that was there with me and all others that would have helped her. She just needs to truly sell the store. This is not her forte. She thinks it is but however, she does not know what she is doing and it clearly shows by the way the store is being run.

# CHAPTER 25

My owners at Subway tell me all the time that they are so great full that they stole me from her because since I have been with them there sales have improved dramatically. The moral of the kids have improved and that helps with the sales as well. Besides they will do more and keep the stores clean if you help them instead of just telling them all the time, so now they all do as I ask and it has improved the store tremendously.

We are puppy sitting tonight and I hope this puppy is not going to cry all night long. He has a bigger dog with him and I don't think that he likes to be alone at night. He is starting to cry being by himself even though there is a bigger dog with him. I don't know if the owners put the dog in the room with them or the daughter but he is in the living room now and he wants to play and be with people. He does not want to just be with the dog. We were out side and playing around the pool and the dog fell inside the pool. We grabbed the dog and dried him off. That poor little shit was shivering so bad, he was scared and cold. This dog is howling all night and I am not going to get any sleep and I have to work a double tomorrow. That is not going to work.

Today I was called by one of my old employees and he told me "that the owner of the Dairy Queen is saying "that I was going around causing trouble last night and asking questions about what she supposedly order for her store from her food distributor." I asked if the food distributor was there because I just wanted to say "hello to the driver as he was a friend of mine from being there for so long." Where was the harm in this?" That was not causing any trouble. Yet one of the employees was outside of her store and smoking but did not wash there hands before serving customers and making products.

My friend ordered something and paid for it so there was nothing wrong in this. The kids that work for her are so ready to walk out on her and she thinks that I am causing the trouble. She seriously needs to look at what she is doing because if the district manager gets a few complaints against her she will not know what happened to her. They will not come from me however, they will come from other customers that have complained to me.

They have asked me how to get a hold of someone and where they would make there complaints known. I just tell them to contact Dairy Queen International on the internet. They could get this information form an 800 telephone number in the directory. I do not think that anyone could not get this information by surfing the internet if they try. Its not too hard these days, so it's not like someone could not find out the information there. It didn't have to come from me so if she were to try and ask me "I would just say, I am sure that they could have gotten it from the internet, after all how many people have a computer these days?" She is the type that runs with a tail between her legs as she can not face up to the person she is complaining about, she just has to go around in a circle like a child.

Today is Sunday and I am working at Subway, it is busy today and Bart and I are working together. He is pretty cool to work with. His friend likes to stick around and I really don't mind because he has been helping us out all day. He has been doing things in the store to make things easier on us all day, at least this way he won't let me pick up anything heavy either. It's funny how the kids understand that I can not pick up anything heavy and the old boss at D Q could not or did not want to understand. That is just because she did not want to understand, not a problem.

My friend Dedee has gotten in touch with me again and she wants to come back and work for us so my manager put her to work for our store and we will see how it works out. I only hope I do not loose out on my hours because I will be upset if I loose because she is there. If this happens, I will go find another job as I do know of a couple other places that are looking for help, and I will go and apply there.

One of the girls that used to work for me didn't seem to friendly today for some reason. She seemed a little on the snobbish side. Like I offended her being around her for some reason and she was in my store, so I was going to say something to her but I didn't as this would cause a problem, so I just left it a lone. I just told her to tell her family that I said "hello and left it at that."

Bob called and wanted to talk to me about meeting him next month. He said "he can not wait to meet me as he is driving and he is as hard as a rock." He said "he is there and can not wait to see me. That when we meet that all he can think of is me licking his cock and putting my lips around it as it grows so big. As I touch him gently and caress him with one finger all over his private parts licking every inch. Making him bigger and bigger, harder and Harder.

This little puppy that we are sitting is adjusting a lot better to his family being away. He still wants to be around people at night but I think that's because the other dog is allowed to get out of his cage at night and he is not. He tried to mark his spot by making his business in his cage the other day and my roommate did not believe me. She cleaned it up while the little one and the big dog were outside.

This little dog is so funny. He thinks he owns the house. He will get in the big dogs cage and drink from the dog's water bottle after watching the big dog drink from it hanging on the side of the cage. He does not have one in his cage. He walks side by side with the big dog like it is his big brother. Let's hope he does not yelp all night again tonight.

Bob called today and wanted to know why I could not meat him until the second week in February. I told him "that my boss was going to Pakistan and that I had to be there for him for all the stores and to watch his house while he was gone because he will not let anyone else in the house." Then he said "I know that your birthday is coming up soon and it is your milestone." I didn't say anything at first and then I called him back and said "Hey, I'm glad you remembered that it is going to be my birthday, do you know exactly how old I am going to be?" He said "Yes, your going to be fifty, and do you know how old I am this year?" I said "Yes, you are fifty five, we are five years apart, and the baby is going to be one on the twenty-eight of the month." Then he said "I hope he knows what he is going through." I said "they don't realize it yet. Not until they are about a year and a half old do they start realizing what parties and things of this nature are all about."

Then he said "I miss you honey, drive careful and take car of my package for me. I will see you soon." He did not seem to think that what was said needed to have an apology of any kind because in his mind he was not wrong. He will never say "I'm sorry to me for what was said."

If I want to make a big deal about it and hold a grudge about it then I need not to meet him and go on with my life. If I want to forgive him and keep on with the relationship and work on our life then that is something that I must work out. He told me that he was going to work on my milestone when we get together because he is not here to make that with me now. He said "that he wants to meet me for dinner and talk before we go to the hotel for the night to retire because we have to talk about some things and we have not seen each other for two months." I did not call because of what was said and I was truly mad at him and I truly did not care if I ever saw him again.

After all the years of being with him, that was unusual for me, because I truly loved him with all my heart and soul. I guess you could tell by the way that I put up my house for sale for him, and everything else that happened along the way like the room-mates.

I was outside of the Subway tonight and the kids were talking to me, when Bart was telling me that he did not want to work with one of the other kids because he did not like the way he treats him. He wanted me to get on the phone and talk to the owner to tell him that this kid was being disrespectful to him, and that he did not want to work with him anymore and that if he had to continue to work with him he would quit. I called the boss and tried to smooth things out and told him that if Quadr was to be working with Bart that he would not work there any longer. Bart is a great worker and I have no problem with him.

I worked with Bart on Sunday and we worked so well together that the day went by fast and before you knew it the day was over. When I told the boss what Quadr was doing he said "he did not even want to work at Subway ," he said " please do me a favor and come over and tell Gail this so that she does not think that I am just telling her something that she does not want to hear."

I told him that "I would tell her anytime that he is the cause of the problem and that she would have to face up to it. She will have to understand that business is business and I love her and Ronny very much. But Quadr is going to take the business down and if that happens then who is going to protect them if something happens to Paul?

While I was outside talking to Paul and getting this problem solved, the kids at the other store called and told me that "one of the customers said that her sandwich rang up at a higher price than what was on the menu and it was on her charge and she wanted to know why?" I asked the young man to do me a favor "as I was not there to just put in the computer the price of a meal-deal and see if that is what rang up instead of what she was to get." He told me" that it was not that price", and I told him "to offer her some chips, and a drink to compensate the price and I would have the owner check the price tomorrow to see what happened." She was okay with that and said "thank-you." I said "Your welcome and sorry about the confusion. She said "She would be back and thank me for taking the time to handle this." I said "that's what I am here for."

While I was outside the store the other kids from Dairy Queen came out and asked me "If I could get him a job if he quit Dairy Queen tonight because he did not like the way the new owner was running the store?" I said "I would call Paul and ask him and see what he says." I called him and he told me to tell "him to come up and talk to him tomorrow around seven pm." He said "he would be there." Then he called Tammy and told her that he quit and that he was locking up the store and that he could not work the store any more tonight. He could not work for her as he thought that she was a poor manager and owner and that the store was dirty and that the paint on the wall was chipped and the refrigerator up front was dirty.

That he was tired of being told to do all the work by looking at the posters on the wall and not being showed correctly as she should. That if the district manager walked into the store at this point that they would tell her to close the doors because they are dirty. Then he proceeded to tell her that Rangy was the only good owner of the store that he worked for and that she should sell the store." She said "I'm sorry you feel that way and is there anything that I can do to keep you?" He said "NO." He asked me "Where can I put the key so she will get it?" I said "Hold on to it so that you can give it back to her when you pick up your check."

He locked up the store and walked out. He wanted to hand me the key and I said "I don't work there any more and I don't' want any responsibility to that store. If something comes up missing she will blame me and I want no part of it what so ever. I am so sorry for what she has done. My customers all know what has happened and are like I cannot believe what she has done to you. They think that she is in the wrong. They have known me for twelve years. I am like family to them.

Like they say "What goes around comes around and I will not do anything to her because I do not want it coming back to bite me in the butt." I believe that she will get what is coming to her by the man above. HE sees all and takes care of everything. What a difference a day makes. He called the other young lady that works with him to have her call Tammy to see if she was going to come in and cover for her as the store was left unattended.

I would have loved to see if she came in and who came into cover it because he just left it operational for someone else to work. She hired this kid name Josh and he is not worth the time of day. I honestly do not know if she listens to anyone when you tell her something. When she first purchased the store I told her that if certain kids came into the store looking for a job do not hire them as they are not Dairy Queen Material. Well guess what she hired him. She refuses to put a help wanted sign in the paper or in the window and weed out the good and the bad help.

She is so desperate for help that she is taking just any one that walks in off the streets and doesn't look at what the problem really is. When she has to deal with the customers complaints then she will have to either let him loose or just give him fewer hours like we did. Some people never learn. This is also part of the reason why Steve quit on her tonight. I really cannot blame him one bit He called me today and told me "that he went over and gave her back the key and picked up his paycheck and that she wanted to know if there was anything that she could do to make him stay?" He said "I told you that you just do not know how to run a store and that is why it is being run down."

The other young lady that was going to quit feels sorry for her so she is going to stay on for a while so she will have some help. I am sorry but she did this to herself. If she would treat people with a little more respect she would get it back then they would not quit on her at the last minute. I am not saying that he was right in leaving the job at the last minute, he should have worked his shift and then told her that he did not want to work for her any more but that is just the way he is.

I ran into Don today and we sat and had breakfast together. That was nice to be able to sit and talk to him. I enjoyed his company at the breakfast table. He had to pick up the boys from school soon, and I asked him to tell them that I said "Hello and I miss them." He said "That they came over to see me at the Dairy Queen and that the young man at the Diary Queen told him that I no longer worked there." He said "Since when she has been here for ever." He said "She quit about two weeks ago, but she works at Subway next door." When he brought the boys over to see me I was not there yet so he said that he would bring them back as they have not seen me in a long time. And they miss me. I said "I miss them too."

I thanked him for the company at the table and wished him a wonderful day. Then I went on about my day. I told him to give me a call and lets take the boys out to a movie or something some time. I would love to have some fun with them. He said that "Christmas was good for them. It was a lot easier this year." I said "Good, I was glad. And how about you, Was it good and easier on you as well? It's not just good and easy for the kids you know you do have to think about yourself."

He just looked at me and smiled. He knew that I understand that it's not easy being mom and dad to the kids and not having leisure time to your-self. There is school work and after school care. There are games and homework and discipline and fun times as well and being just one parent it is not always easy. I asked him "if he knew anything about publishing? " He said "No but he had a friend that does and he will get me in touch with him and I can talk to him so that will be no problem." Then he asked me "why." I said "Because I am writing a book and I am just about finished with it and I do not have a publisher or do not know how to go about getting it publish nor do I know how to get it sponsored to get it published."

He told me that he would get him in touch with me and he could explain it or help me. I told him thank you. He is really a nice guy. There should be more like him around. I truly would not mind going out with him if he asked me out. He just has never asked me. I don't know why.

Today is Thursday and Bob called again. He wanted to know if I can get off on the beginning of February in stead of the second week in February. My sister that lives in GA. Is having an engagement party for her daughter in the end of January and I just might call and ask him if he wants to meet then instead. He might not because that is the baby's birth date as well and he might say that he can not get away that weekend. I asked him why he doesn't bring the baby down for me to meet him this time. He told me he might he was not sure.

Chris, the baby, will be a year old January 28th. Bob called me up to tell me that he finally called him "Pa Pa" today on the phone and with the sitter at home. He is so happy. I asked him "who will he be calling "Ma Ma.? " He said "No one there is no "Ma Ma there now." I said "when he starts to talk he will be soon calling the sitter "ma ma" as there is no one else there that the child knows. He did not want to talk about that. I just said "Have a nice day." He said "I will call you later." I said "be careful is nasty up there. I will talk to you soon."

I was at work last night and the girl that was to work yesterday did not show or call so the owner called her to see if she was going to come in today. She said "She was sick and that she was going to come in today and that she was sorry about yesterday." This store is very busy and you cannot do it with just one person. When I got to work at night for some reason, my night crew young man did not show or call and this is not like him in the least. His mother called and said "That he had just left the house and would I have him call as soon as he got to work." I said "Yes, I surely will.

He should be here any minute. Well he never showed or called all night. I called and called him all night. I left a message on the phone and told him I did not care what time of the night it was to please call me and let me know if he was all right because we have a special friendship between co-workers that you usually do not have with adults and teenagers. He finally called me and told me that he was okay and what was going on and that he would be in to work on the next night and would I call the owner and smooth things over as he could not afford to loose his job.

I called the owner and talked to him because he knows that the kids get along with me so well and we can talk about anything and everything that is bothering them no matter what. If it is work or non work related issues it can be talked about and we discuss what might be bothering them. If I can be of assistance to them then I will do what I can, if I can't then I will let them know and try to direct them in the proper way to where they need to go.

I think that is why we get along so well and I respect there opinions as young adults as well. I might not agree with some of them, but I respect them. We always discuss them. We work together well and share the duties together not making one person having to do all the work. That makes the difference.

I work in another store and I have a young lady that I was working with whom I thought was a very close friend. She all of a sudden stops talking to me. I could not figure out what I did wrong. When I called her to talk to her she would hang up the phone or just avoid me. When it came time for us to be on the schedule together she would always ask the other young lady to work in her place. I went in the other day and I was given a note to read.

This is the kind of respect that I have from these kids. She writes: First of all I want to deeply apologize for the way I've been behaving with you. I don't want you to think that I'm a bad person. It's just that I have some issues that I have to deal with. I have been in so much pressure for almost 5 years that I am about to give up. Please don't hate me (with a sad face). You're a good friend and I'm doing you wrong. I'm ashamed to call you 'cause I don't really know how to express myself if I'm on the phone. Since I got to America, I never saw anybody that I could see as a Mother figure but you. I care a lot about you, so I will apologize once again. Please forgive me. I love you,. P S Merry Christmas and Happy New Year Simone.

I wrote her back a letter and told her that I accepted her apology and that I always thought of her as a friend. The fact that she thought of me as a mother figure was a very high honor and I was extremely proud of that. I would be very proud if she would celebrate my golden birthday with me as it was coming up this weekend, and if she would like to I would appreciate it if she would be there. I had no problem with her being around me and I love her very much. Whatever was bothering her she could always talk to me and we can figure it out some way. There is always a way to do this. Just to give me a call. I have not heard from her as yet.

My birthday is in two days. I will try and call her tomorrow and see if she wants to get together and see what her plans are. Maybe a bunch of us can go to the movies or something. I don't drink so that would not interest me in the least. My one sister wants to take me out to dinner and I have no idea what my other sisters are going to do.

They have not contacted me as to what they want to do if anything as of yet. If they do not want to do anything, well that is quite okay with me. I will still be here. I will just keep on going as I have to, one day at a time. My other friend's birthday is one day before mine. How ironic is that. We get along just fine. As a matter of fact we are pretty good friends and he is a guy. Just a few years younger than I but that's okay. Still he's okay, he's still my friend. Maybe all of us should get together and go to a midnight movie for both of our birth days. Let me see if I can set it up.

Today is Friday and I am now at the Subway next to the Dairy Queen working on my second shift. One of the kids came in and asked me "If I could give him a sub and let him pay for it later and I had to tell him that my boss would not allow me to do this." I will not loose the respect from him or my job because I gave away a sub to one of the kids next door. My boss and his wife and son came in to give me a birthday card and ask me to meet them for breakfast on Sunday morning because they love me so much.

There is no way I will mess this up. I help him out when he is in trouble and when I am in need of extra hours he is there to help me. Why would I mess up this relationship with him? I watch the family pets when they go away because his son does not trust any one else to watch them as he feels that anyone else would not take care of them as I would and love them as much. Honestly they are like my second family. When he came in I made him a little pizza and his mom was going to make it but then she said "Well you go ahead because he loves you so much that anything that you do is special to him."

I have investments with Bob's insurance company that he works for and when I called to check on how to change my beneficiary I could not get any answers from the company. I was told that I did not have any investments with them. I said "what do you mean I do not have any investments with you. I have several in the amount of $50,000.00 and I would like to know what is going on. I want some answers as to what is happening in this company now or I will have IRS on you tomorrow. I said my agents name is Bob Jones and I want to know what is happening now. You can reach me at and I left my phone number. I called the agent and I am dealing with him." He cannot get any answers from them either.

This is very upsetting and I told him that at this point he can pull my money out of his company and give me a cashier's check for the amount. Again I intend to put the money in a secure place like a bank and I will not have to worry about it." He did not like it too well but he really can not say anything as it is my money and my investment. I also told him that if I can't get any answers on the phone I can imagine what it is like if I needed the money now.

I want to secure my investments and make sure that I do not loose any thing as when I brought it up to his attention one of the things that he had to say of concerns was that his sister has investments with his company as well. I said "I am not worried so much about your sister's investments at this point as I can not loose anymore money. I wanted to check and make sure that I had a certificate for the amount of money that you owed me and get a beneficiary change form which has made this into a night mare. He cannot get any answers from the company and I am having just as much trouble.

I will have to go to the FEC and see what kind of answers I can get in order to see where I stand with these certificates. I do remember him telling me that they just opened another office just around the corner from where I work and I can get that office address and go there and find out what is happening, if I cannot get any answers from him. I am truly upset with this and if I have to pull these out I will and do something else with my money.

As I was driving on the highway today on this beautiful sunny day to visit my niece for her Engagement party this weekend, I got caught up in traffic from a horrible accident. I sat in this traffic for an hour as the officials tried to clear up the traffic. All you could do was to listen to the radio and not get stressed out. As I thought about the time I would be spending at the dinner with Bob, I thought I better call him and tell him I might be a little late as the accident put me behind. I was meeting him in Savannah. I called him and let him know that I might be a little late but I would do my best to make up the time and try not to be late.

I drove all day to make the time as I really didn't want to be late. I was so looking forward to going to the hotel and refreshing first to be with him for dinner and putting on a special dress for dinner. When I got to the hotel I got the room and I did not have time to refresh and change so I just used the facilities and went to the restaurant. As I got to the restaurant I saw Bob outside and then he went back inside. He did not see me pull up. This was good as my approach was working. He called me and asked me if I would have time to get the hotel before coming to the restaurant and I told him I was not sure as he was coming from another state.

I went into the restaurant and approached his table and he said "to me have a seat." I said "could we start over, I wanted to do something?" I walked away from the table and then walked back and asked him "is this seat taken?" He said "NO." I said "may I join you?" He said "Please do." I said "sometimes please don't be so fast to just say something before I can say something to you because you never know what I may be planning or wanting to say to you." I got up and planted a big kiss on his mouth in the restaurant and I know he does not like public affection but I told him to enjoy it anyway. I told him that some things would have to change. Like a little affection in public once in a while wouldn't hurt now and then.

We had dinner and then we left. We went to the hotel and spent the night and got up the next morning. We always have a wonderful time together when we are together. We have a lot of talking to do and this is how we can get it settled. Away from every one else, where no-one else will put there p's and q's in to and try and tare us apart from what we really want. It really is our decision on whether we stay together or not.

He said "he will be back down next week for a surprise visit to the office that is currently holding the investment with the company that he works for and he is going to surprise them to find out what is going on because no one can get any answers on the phone as to what we want to know. "I told" him that if he cannot get any answers from the company that I want all my investments pulled out. And I want my money in a cashiers check soaps to be able to put it some where else, where it is a little safer and I will tell my sister to do the same." I asked him "if his boss is not worried about the situation as well.' He said "yes he is, he is very worried because there is a lot of money involved here and he does not want all these investments taken out." Bob would also have to contact all the other clients that he had at that time and have them pull theirs out as well. That is one headache I would not want. I do not envy him at all.

We got up the next morning and went to breakfast at the local Cracker Barrel. I don't really care for the place but he likes it so we went. Then we had to go on the road. He called me on the cell and told me "the exit I had to get off and told me he would see me soon and that he missed me already."

I left him and headed for the engagement party. He could not come with me. I was at the party house for two days. It was my sister's house. I got there on Saturday night and I had to leave on Sunday because I had to be back on Monday. My sister needed help as I was walking in the house in the kitchen with cooking, so she put me right to work. That's okay what are sisters' for? We help each other all the time. I just asked her what she needed and I did what she said. The party came out great. My niece loved it and that is all that matters. We brought it all to the club house and then set it up and Franc JR. set up the party house it turned out very well.

She received some very nice gifts and a lot of wine. We teased them that they were going to become a little bit of win-o-s and of course they joke a long with us on this. They are just two beautiful kids. Then most of the adults left and the younger ones stayed for a little while longer. The next morning my sister, her husband, my niece, and myself went out to breakfast and then I went on the road back to home. That was a long trip back as I love being with them. It truly makes me want to be up there with them. It is so beautiful.